The Tow of Quar

GW01271812

A quiet corner of the
Parish of Bolton-le-Moors

The old Chimney and the reservoir are all
that remains of Quarlton Vale Print Works

SECOND EDITION

Publication No 21   James J. Francis

No 21 The Township of Quarlton
James J Francis
Published by Turton Local History Society
Second Edition September 2009
ISBN 978-1-904974-98-7

TURTON LOCAL HISTORY SOCIETY

Turton Local History Society exists to promote an interest in history by discussion, research and record. It is particularly concerned with the history of the former Urban District of Turton and its constituent ancient townships of Bradshaw, Edgworth, Entwistle, Harwood, Longworth, Quarlton and Turton. Meetings are held from September to May inclusive, at 7.30pm on the third Tuesday of the month at the Barlow Institute, Edgworth. Visitors are welcome.

Previous publications are listed on the inside front cover. In recognition of the years of research undertaken and as a matter of courtesy and good academic practice, it is expected that due acknowledgement will be made to the author and Turton Local History Society when any further use is made of the contents of this and previous publications.

CONTENTS

ILLUSTRATIONS

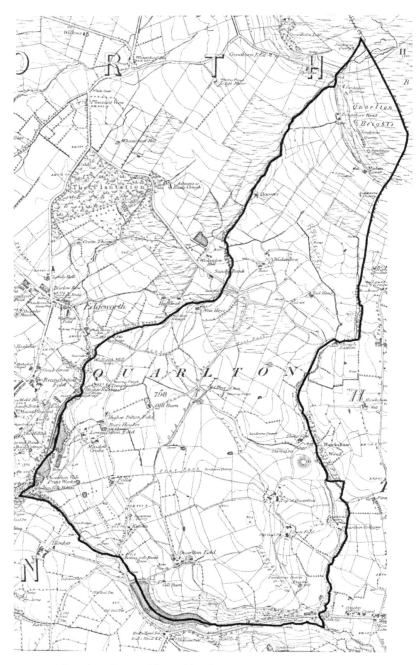

Quarlton Township outlined on the 6 inch 1850 OS map.

Chapter I   THE EARLY DAYS

One of the old townships of the ancient Parish of Bolton-le-Moors, Quarlton lies to the north-east of the Parish up to the boundary with the Parish of Bury and the Township of Tottington Lower End.

Being on the slopes of Quarlton Heights and Holcombe Moor, the ground rises from about 650 feet above sea level at Quarlton Vale up to 1,250 feet at the northern junction with the Edgworth and Tottington Townships. One of the smaller townships of Bolton Parish, it has an area of 798 acres being of a triangular shape bounded by the Quarlton Brook on the west, Hawkshaw Brook on the east and Walves Brook to the south.

The general geological form of this area is of fertile valley floors and thinly soiled hilly areas over boulder clay and sedimentary bedrocks. These sedimentary deposits vary between millstone grits on the north-eastern side of the township and shales to the west. Coal measures exist but due to the upheaval and subsequent erosion when the first ranges of the Pennine Hills were formed, the seams are of the Lower Coal Measures and it is the Mountain Mine Series that has been worked locally, initially from outcrops.

No evidence of the Stone Age has been found in Quarlton but traces of occupation have been discovered on Holcombe Moor at Bull Hill, a little to the north-east of the Quarlton boundary. These finds included arrow heads and other flints used as tools and/or weapons. There are positive signs of early settlement in the adjacent area of Belmont and the Stone Circle on Turton Heights, so it is quite likely that Bronze and Iron Age itinerant graziers and hunters roamed the Quarlton slopes although no actual evidence can be found of settlement in the Township itself right up to the time of the Roman invasion.

The Romans invaded Britain from the south-east in 43 AD with Brigantia -including Lancashire - having a political arrangement of semi-independence. This started to break down by 70 AD when northern England became openly hostile leading to Roman troops invading Brigantia. In order to control the area, forts were built at the more important communication points with military roads constructed to allow quick movement between these defence positions. By the end of the first century a road was established between Mamucium (Manchester) and Bremetennacum (Ribchester) which ran through the south-west of the eventual area of Quarlton.

Local excavations have proved the line of the road south of Knotts, Pallet and Meadowcrofts but the crossing of Quarlton Brook into the Edgworth area is not yet established. The excavations recorded a road of about seven to eight yards in breadth made up of a base of larger stones filled in with smaller fragments. Although minor Roman objects have been found adjacent to the road, including pieces of a Roman pot, and a small hoard of Roman coins in an Affetside wall, we have little evidence of

Roman life in the area. It has been suggested that the distance from Manchester would justify a local military resting station but nothing has been found to date.

The roughly straight line from Affetside seems to have been diverted slightly westerly with the building of the Walves Reservoir, but there is an ancient diversion at the foot of Knotts Brow where the Roman Road crosses the Walves Brook and the current line of the road turns almost 45 degrees to the north from the proven line. Could this diversion have been brought about by a medieval enclosure forming Pallet, Meadowbarn and Pelton Fold farms requiring a joint occupation road through Quarlton rather than on its southerly border?

Of the Romano-British there is little evidence apart from a hand corn-grinding quern found on Bradshaw Road in 1963 - could this have been produced from local gritstone found in Querndon?

The name of Quarlton includes 'ton' of Saxon origin and D Mills suggests the name could be a corruption of the Old English 'cweon dun' - the hill of querns or millstones. From Quernedon, Querndone, Quordone in the late 1300s, later as Quarnadon or Quarnton developing into Quarlton in the 17th Century.

At the Great Inquest of King John in 1212, Edgworth was held of the King by William de Radcliffe, which included at this time what we know of today as the Township of Quarlton and a large proportion of Entwistle. The Entwistle part was later given to Robert de Entwistle on his marriage to William de Radcliffe's daughter, while the Township of Edgworth was granted to the Traffords. The Radcliffes held Quarlton to themselves from 1305.

Because of this background, the freeholders of Quarlton, Entwistle and Edgworth all held rights of common to Edgworth Moor and qualified for awards of land on the eventual enclosure of Edgworth Moor in 1795.

The Quarlton Manor estate of the Radcliffes was, from 1305, supplemented by the Birches Farms on a long lease (3 shillings per annum chief rent) from the Bradshaws of Bradshaw - explaining why the estate maps of 1620 and 1725 included the Birches part of Bradshaw.

The adjacent Townships of Tottington Lower and Higher Ends were included in the Barony of the de Montbegons and in 1225, Roger de Montbegon, who was mesnes Lord under the Lacys, gave on his death to the Monk Bretton Monastery in Yorkshire the whole forest of Holcombe and the pasture within, viz, *'as far as the forest extends in length and breadth towards Querendon* (Quarlton) *and by the bounds of the forest up to Lonschahehevet* (Longshaw Head) *and thence across the path divides into Holcomhehevet* (Holcombe Head) *up to Pilgrimscrosschahe* (Pilgrims Cross Shaw) *and thence descending to the road which leads through the middle of Tittlesow* (Tittleshaw) etc, etc'

As with the Forest of Rossendale, these woodlands would have been cleared and settled by the end of the 15th Century but the above bequest suggests that similar woodlands existed at these higher levels of Quarlton and Longshaw Head in the 13th Century.

The hunting rights and privileges were the right of the Crown and in 1304 the King in his gratitude to Richard de Radecliffe for his services in the Scottish Wars granted him and his heirs free warren in all the desmesne lands in Radcliffe and Querendon. Quarlton in the 14th Century seems to have been an ideal hunting park and this grant of free warren probably formed the future base for the Holcombe Harriers.

Being a Township in the ancient Parish of Bolton-le-Moors, Quarlton was responsible for paying tithes, and in 1305 the tithe for Edgworth and Quarlton set to Richard of Radcliffe was ii marks, as against the tithe from Turton of iv marks and ix shillings. Both Edgworth and Quarlton at this time must have been sparsely occupied rough areas probably not yet fully cleared of old woodland and scrub. However, in the 1332 Exchequer Lay Subsidy Rolls is recorded the name of Elia de Quernedone as paying tax, which at this time was levied on a person's movable items at a rate of one tenth of their value.

The Radcliffes held Quarlton along with Smithills and other lands until the marriage of Joanna Radcliffe to Ralph Barton c1467. The family continued to live on the Barton estate at Holme-by-Newark in Nottinghamshire until their son John married Cecily Radcliffe in 1486 to cement the two family estates under the Barton name. John Barton, after bringing his family up to Smithills, sought religious seclusion in later life, leaving his son Andrew (1498-1549) as head of the family. Andrew remained at Smithills, as did his son Ralph Barton (1525-1592) and grandson Randall Barton (1556-1611).

An Inquisition was taken at Bolton, on 15th April 1612 after the death of Randle Barton Esq. He was *'seized in fee of...and 8 messuages, 100 acres of land, 20 acres of meadow, 200 acres of pasture and 1000 acres of moor, furze and heath in Quarneton. Randall Barton died 10th December, 1611, his heir was Thomas Barton, his son, aged at the time of taking this Inquisition 28 years or more. The messuages etc in Querneton are held of the King as of the late Priory of St John of Jerusalem in Socage by fealty and 16d rent and are worth £3.'* The lists of Lancashire possessions of the Knights of St John of Jerusalem (Hospitalers) of 1291-2 includes Edgewick (Edgworth) which at this time included Quarlton. The 1540 lists of rentals of the Free Tenants of the Hospitalers includes Quernton (Quarlton) of Andrew Barton for the Lordship of Querneton at 16 pence. Subsequent lists do not include Quarlton so we must assume the Hospitalers sold their interest some time between 1540 and 1558.

The *'Clitherow Court Rolls'* of 14th May 1541 note *'Letter of Attorney of Andrew Barton of Smythyls Esq appointing Andrew Knolls of Querneton his lawful attorney to do his business and appear for him in Tottington Court given at Smythyls on the last day of April 1533.'* This suggests that in the mid-16th Century the Bartons' Quarlton Manor included a portion of Tottington Township as well as the Birches area of Bradshaw. This area is shown on the 1620 Map east of the Quarlton boundary and is land currently part of Hawkshaw Farm.

Randall Barton's son, Sir Thomas Barton became head of the family on Randall's death in 1611 and seemed to take a specific interest in Quarlton by becoming the first recorded Hunt Master of the Holcombe Hounds in 1617 when he attended King James I on his visit to Hoghton Tower; he was described as Sir Thomas Barton of Quarlton. On August 16th of that visit it was recorded *'The King hunting, a great companie killed afore dinner a brace of staggs, verrie hott so he went to dinner. In the afternoon hunted ye hare'*. The King was so pleased with the deep mouthed Holcombe Hounds that their owner was graciously given the Royal Warrant to hunt over twelve Townships and the privilege of wearing the scarlet livery of the King. With this background, we can understand the association of the Holcombe Hunt with Quarlton Township over the next three centuries.

Chapter II   SIR THOMAS BARTON'S MANOR OF QUARLTON

Soon after his father's death, Sir Thomas Barton, in seeking to redefine his various lands, in 1620 had plans drawn for his Quarlton and Horwich Manors.

The plan of his Quarlton estate is headed - *'The place of Quarnton, belonging to the right Worshipfull Sir Thomas Barton of Smithills, Knight, Taken by William Senior, Professor of Mathematiques, Anno Domina 1620.'*

This is a remarkably descriptive plan showing quite clearly the Birches estate within the Bradshaw Township to the south of the Walves Brook and a small section of Tottington Lower End Township to the east of the Hawkshaw Brook in the vicinity of Hawkshaw Farm.

There are pictorial positions of messuages (farmhouses) which we can reasonably assume denote farms with buildings and associated fields. All the fields are marked with the tenant's name and generally the field name.

Although we refer to Barton's Quarlton Manor as the whole Township, there is one exception and that is land owned directly of the Lord of the Manor (Sir Thomas Barton) on a long lease (probably 999 years). In 1620 this was owned by Adam Warburton and was in two locations, that area we know now as Meadowcrofts Farm and a smaller area on the north-west boundary of the township now known as Barons. The Meadowcrofts area rent was *'a paire of spurs'*, while the Barons area was subject to a ground rent of 1s-4d.

On the northerly tip of the Township is an area of 25a.2r.32p denoted *'The common to the water fall'*. This description probably refers to the Quarlton Brook falling rapidly down a small ravine. We have no record of the rights of this common which would have been additional to the rights enjoyed on Edgworth Moor by ancient rights.

The messuages detailed on the plan include farms now known as Top of Quarlton, Lower Fold, Quarlton Fold, Knotts, Pallet, Pelton Fold, Wickenlow and Maken Tower. These are probably the eight messuages mentioned in Randle Barton's will of 1612, which suggests that the other land holdings were farmed by people with farms outside Quarlton Township or who lived in cottages attached to the above mentioned eight messuages, eg Top of Quarlton and Quarlton Fold. There was a Thomas Warburton who died 31st August 1634 at Stubbins who held two messuages in Quarlton of Sir Thomas Barton and other tenants may well have lived in adjacent Townships. There do not appear to be any cottages along Bury Road at this time and the road through Hawkshaw was not then built.

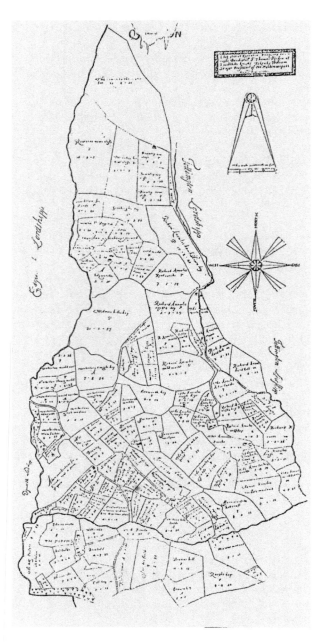

Sir Thomas Barton's Quarlton Estate Map of 1620.

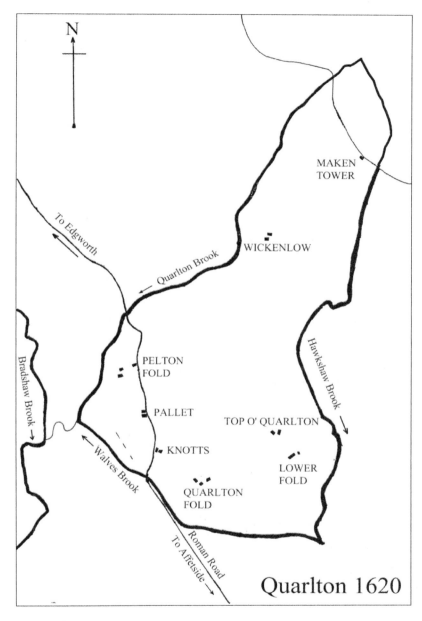

Quarlton Farms marked on Sir Thomas Barton's Map of 1620.

Further study of the 1620 map describes the various holdings as follows:-

Later known Names	Quoted Tenants		A	R	P
Top of Quarlton	Richard Knowles		63	2	21
Lower Fold	Thomas Knowles		52	1	17
Quarlton Fold	Farnworth		47	0	38
Knotts	Widow John & William Stones		24	1	26
Pallet	Bramley		12	2	18
Pelton Fold	Warburton		33	3	7
Wickenlow	Thurston Greenhough		30	2	8
Maken Tower	Bramley		8	3	19
Land only	Widow Hills		32	0	7
Land only	Horrocks		9	1	7
Land only	Rosterne		16	3	0
Land only	John Jones		2	2	5
Free ground	Adam Warburton	(Estimate)	15	0	0
	Ditto	(Estimate)	3	1	20
Common			25	2	36
			---	---	---
Sub Total			378	0	39
Less estimate of land in Hawkshaw			11	2	11
			---	---	---
Total			366	2	28

It is interesting to note that Adam Warburton's holding which became known as Meadowcrofts had an early datestone of 1620.

The actual area of Quarlton Township is 798 Statute Acres, so allowing for local surveying errors, the total acreage of the Township on the 1620 map is most likely measured in the large Cheshire Acre - being equal to approximately 2.15 Statute Acres.

On this 1620 map it is interesting to see that most of the fields are marked A, M or P which would indicate arable, meadow or pasture. The arable fields would be ploughed and tilled for growing corn, either oats or barley, the meadows would be for long term grass growth, primarily mown for hay as winter feed and the pastures for grazing throughout the year. We have no record of a typical lease of the time but the requirements would have been to limit acreages in arable land, and to ensure that all hay and straw was consumed on the farm and all manure generated spread back on the land. The proportions of arable, meadow and pasture vary for each holding but pasture areas are the larger being generally a half of their totals.

South-west
facing wing,
1999.

Plaster plaque of Richard
Knowles and his wife Ann
1670, subsequently moved by
Sir Lees Knowles to his
Pendlebury home.

North-east
facing rear of
building to the
yard 1909.

Top of Quarlton.

East facing
front of
main
building,
now
forming
three
cottages.

Door lintel of Thomas
Knowles 1627.

Rear of end
cottage, nearer
the old barn
site.

Lower Fold.

The Will of Thurstone Greenhalghe of Quarlton dated 1574 is interesting because it describes the property of a Quarlton husbandman of the time. It is probable that this Thurstone Greenhalgh was the grandfather of Thurston Greenough noted on the 1620 Quarlton map as holding what we now know as Wickenlow, then having 30 acres (64 Statute Acres). Names were generally passed on verbally and different spellings are common in old records. The appraisal was done by Richard Knowles, Hugh Warburton, Ellis Farnworth and Andrew Knowles (all contemporary Quarlton names) on 3rd April 1574.

Heading the appraisal are 3 oxen valued £7, used for pulling the ploughs and other implements rather than the 3 horses at £5 which would be used for riding and light draught work. His cattle including 6 cows, 1 bull, 3 heifers, 2 twinter steers (two winters old), 5 stirks and calves were valued at £22. He had 10 sheep at £2 and 2 young swine, hens and geese at 10 shillings. Meal, meat and corn were valued at £5, but at the end of April winter feeding would have taken most of his meal and corn. His implements including *'wains, ploughs and arrowes and other tools necessary for the husbandman'* were valued at £3, with stone troughs at 10 shillings. Household goods included brass and pewter etc at 4sh, arcs, chests etc 3sh, bedding etc 4sh, rayment for the body, sacks and one window sheet 1sh, with flesh, butter and cheese at 1sh. In all a £58 valuation.

It can be seen that, although having quite a large holding, his household furnishings with one curtain are quite rudimentary but typical of this period.

The 1620 map shows very few roads, which seem to be limited to the ancient highway along the Roman Road to Edgworth and its junction with the southerly end of what became known as Old Ben Lane. Undoubtedly some occupation roads were in being but it seems from an Indenture of 11th April, 1629 that the way from Richard Knowles' Top of Quarlton to the Edgworth Common (on which he would have tenant's rights) was not agreed with his neighbours. Richard's son, Andrew pays seventeen shillings for a right of way for ever across the Hill's holding to the Edgworth Common at a *'gate caled the lomes gate'*.

In the absence of full details it is difficult to be precise on the number of inhabitants in Quarlton at this time but the Protestation Returns of 1642 give us a guide. These include persons being eighteen years or older and are recorded as William Barn (probably Baron); James Brandwood; Arthur and Raphe Bromileye; Ralph Brooke; Christopher Cotes; Ellis and Henry Haworth; George Horwich; Adam Horrocke; Francis, James, Richard and Henry Knowles; Robert Smythe and Thomas and William Warburton. These include most of the 1620 tenants except the Stones and Hills.

Quarlton Fold farmhouse prior to demolition in 1990.

Farmhouse demolition showing the 'heck' screen to the fireplace with Mr Herbert Ramwell.

Section of an internal timber framed wall with 'wattle and daub' infill.

Quarlton Fold.

The 1666 Hearth Tax Return is a better guide with four residences with two hearths each, those of Robert Knowles, Thomas Knowles, George Bromiley and Jane

Pendleton (possibly Top of Quarlton, Quarlton Fold, Pallet and Knotts) and thirteen with one hearth, namely Howarth, Ellis Hill, Ellis and John Farnworth, John and Daniel Stones, Edward Horrocks, Thurston and Thomas Greenhalgh, William Entwistle, William Haworth, Ralph Bromiley and Richard Royd.

The 1678 Poll Tax Return is however more to the point and defines families as well as single persons and was levied at one shilling per head. They are listed:-

Peter Knowles, his wife and son Andrew	3
Samuel Pendleton, his wife and two children	4
Widow Pikrin	1
Anne Bromiley	1
John Bradshaw	1
Thomas Knowles Senr. and his wife	2
Thomas Knowles Jnr. and his wife	2
John Farnworth, his wife and daughter	3
James Longworth and Mary his daughter	2
Ellis Hill, his wife and Dorothy his daughter	3
Richard Hill and his wife	2
John Stones and his wife	2
Widow Stones and Daniel her son	2
James Farnworth	1
Ellis Farnworth and his wife	2
Arhur Bromiley and Ellin his sister	2
Thomas Greenhalgh and his wife	2
William Entwistle and his wife	2
John Horrocks	1
John Coatts	1
John Barlow and his wife	2
Thomas Stone, his wife and three children	_5_
	46 shillings

Richard Hill was *the 'Colector for ye Hamblet of Quarlton'* and Thomas Stones the Assessor.

Included in this total are fifteen families and seven single persons. The 1620 map denoted nine messuages (including Meadowcrofts). We can assume that either of two things have happened since 1620; that more farmsteads have been built and/or cottages have been added to the existing farms - we do know that twelve farmsteads are noted on the next known map of 1727.

Knotts 1940.

Knotts 1975.

Pallet Farm
c1900, home
of the Walken
family.

Knotts and Pallet Farms.

Pelton Fold Farmhouse
1975.

Living room fireplace
bressummer beam and
'heck' during extensive
renovations.

Farmhouse after
renovation 1999.

Pelton Fold.

Wickenlow:
south facing front of
farmhouse 1976.

Wickenlow:
living room
with fireplace
bressummer and
'heck' 1999.

Site of Maken
Tower: the
ruined
foundations of
which were last
seen c1945.

Not on the 1620 map is Barons (then owned by Adam Warburton) which we know from a 1649 Indenture was sold by Thomas Warburton to Lawrence Horrocks - and stated to be late in the tenure of William Baron. Lawrence Horrocks sold the small farm to William Entwistle in 1674 just in time for him and his wife to pay the Poll Tax in Quarlton. We also know of a date-stone 1660 at Red Earth (set upside down as a quoin in the barn) suggesting this was also a new messuage built since 1620. Longshaw Head could also have been built in this period, as a Survey of the Manor of Tottington 1686 tracing the Township Boundaries notes *'A place called Longshaw Head'*.

Sir Thomas Barton's heir was his only child, Grace Barton, who in 1622 married Henry Belasyse. Henry died in 1647 before either his father or father-in-law and the marriage arrangements for his heir Thomas were made by Sir Thomas Barton. Thomas, who became 2nd Viscount Fauconberg, inherited the Smithills, Horwich and Quarlton estates as well as Newburgh Priory where he lived. The son of Thomas's brother, Sir Rowland Belasyse, also Thomas, became the 3rd Viscount Fauconberg and inherited all the estates including the Quarlton Manor. He died in 1718, but in 1717 Catholics were required to register their name and landholdings with the Clerk of the Peace and under *'The Manor and Lordship of Quarlton with its rights and appurtenances'* were detailed:

1 *'Severall Cheif Rents paid by the Free Holders, amounting to 1s-4d and a paire of spurs per annum.'* (These would be Barons and Meadowcrofts)

2 *'Messuage let to Andrew Knowles for lives of himself and Robert and Sarah his children at £1-13s-4d rent, a day mowing and a day shearing in the demesne of Smithills, eleven loads of turf leading from Edgberdean with a cart or wagon and 5s-2d boons; consideration £20.'*

3 *'Messuage let to William Hutchinson for lives of himself, Mary his wife and Thomas Knowles at £1-3s-4d rent, three hens and 5s-10d boons; consideration £160.*

4 *'Messuage let by Sir Rowland Belasyse to Elizabeth Hill for lives of herself and Henry and Ellis her children at 11s-8d rent, two hens and 3s boons; consideration £41. This tenement & Ellis Farnworths payes besides the sum of 1s-8d to the Crowne for the priviledge of digging turf in the common.'*

5 *'Messuage let to Ellis Farnworth for lives of William, John and Ellis his sons at £1-3s-10d rent and 5s-10d boons; consideration £100.*

6 *'Messuage let to John Stones for lives of himself, Joseph his son and Thomas, son of John Barlow at 5s-10d rent and 1s-8d boons; consideration £20.*

7 *'Messuage let to Arthur Bromiley for lives of Margaret his wife and James and John, sons of James Whittley at 9s rent, three boon hens and 4s-9d boons; consideration £15.'*

8 *Messuage let by Earl Fauconberg to Alice Bromiley for lives of Arthur, John and Ellen her children at 8s rent, a hen and 1s-7d boons; consideration £13.*

9 *'Messuage let to Andrew Bury for lives of William his son and Ann and Alice, daughters of Andrew Knowles at 18s rent, four boon hens and 6s-4d boons; consideration £125.'*

10 *'Messuage let by Sir Rowland Belasyse to William Entwistle for lives of himself and Thomas and William his sons at 15s rent, three hens and 5s-10d boons; consideration £52.'*

11 *'Messuage let to Adam Horrocks for lives of John his son and Adam and James, sons of William Horrocks at 9s rent, a day shearing and 6s boons; consideration £4'.*

12 *'Messuage let to John Entwistle for lives of Thomas his son and Edward and Alice, children of Thomas Barlow at 14s-8d rent and all such harriots as by the Customs of the Town or Place shall become due.'*

13 *'Messuage let to David Whitehead for lives of himself and Jonathon and Thomas his sons at 5s-10d rent and 1s-8d boons; consideration £10.'*

This indicates 14 separate farm holdings (including Barons and Meadowcrofts). The earlier 1678 Poll Tax returns indicate 15 families and 7 single persons. This difference must be made up by some farms having two or more holdings, eg Top of Quarlton and Quarlton Fold, and others with additional cottages.

Thomas Belasyse, the 4th Viscount Fauconberg succeeded in 1718 and sold his Quarlton Estate in 1723 to William Wright of Mottram St Andrew, Cheshire, who already owned land in Sharples. Viscount Fauconberg also had some copyhold land in Tottington, six acres held by Andrew Knowles – probably with Top of Quarlton and holding this Tottington land later as part of his Hawkshaw Farm. The second Tottington holding was six acres held by Christopher Horrocks which probably made up Clough Bottom Farm (marked on the 1620 map).

The Wright family came from near Nantwich in Cheshire, the heirs from the late 16th century were named Laurence for five generations. Laurence Wright who inherited in 1582 lived initially at Nantwich, but later at Offerton Hall.

William Wright succeeded to the Wright estates on his father Henry's death in 1711 and that of Uncle Laurence in 1712. He purchased Mottram St Andrew in 1738 which became the family home for 150 years. It was a few years after inheriting the Wright estates that William bought the Quarlton Manor in 1723. His purchase may have been influenced by knowing the Bradshaw-Isherwoods, his neighbours of Marple Hall who were the Lords of the Manor of Bradshaw.

Grace Barton, Sir Thomas Barton's heir: 1622.

Sir Richard Belasyse 1632-1699, of Smithills, Quarlton and Newburgh Priory.

Chapter III   WILLIAM WRIGHT'S QUARLTON

A few years after the purchase of the Quarlton Manor, William Wright had a plan of the estate drawn up by Matts. Aston in 1727. This is similar in detail to the Barton 1620 map but unfortunately no tenants are named apart from the two directly held farms of Barons and Meadowcrofts which were held by Thomas Entwistle and Mr Meadowcroft respectively. The land to the east in Tottington Lower End Township is no longer within the Wright estate and it would appear that at the time of sale this section was taken over by the Knowles family to add to their Hawkshaw Farm which in the 1794 Survey is owned by Andrew and Robert Knowles.

The roads were by now better defined with the Affetside to Edgworth road taking the now familiar route via Knotts brow. What later became Old Ben Lane is shown running from the top of Knotts brow up to Old Heyes with a branch to Quarlton Fold. There are some fields with the same name as they had a hundred years previously but quite a number of the larger fields are split up into smaller areas, an example being Longshaw Head Farm. On the 1620 map the previous large single field now forms six smaller closes. This division is associated with additional farmsteads; in 1727 Sheepcote is now formed to the east of Top o' Quarlton, with Old Heyes in the centre, Red Head or Red Earth in the north-east and Longshaw Head in the north, adjacent to the lane we now know as Moor Bottom Road, and a neighbour of the older Maken Tower - over the years referred to as Morgan Tower or Manken Tower and perhaps named after the Makin family who lived at Wickenlow in 1740.

The first indication of coal mining is noted by the names of three fields to the west of Top of Quarlton called 'Great Cole Pit Field', 'Long Cole Pit Field' and 'Little Cole Pit Field'. This is near the area where the Upper Mountain Mine seam outcropped and the coal might be worked simply by digging out. The seam slopes from west to east at an angle of approximately 20% so that after digging out as deep as practicable, shafts would need to be sunk to get to the coal bed that was dipping steeper than the slope of the natural ground. At these deeper levels drainage soughs (or tunnels) would be required to remove water from the workings. There are also two fields north-west of Wickenlow called 'Little Pit Field' and 'Great Pit Field' but we have no record of coal mining in this locality and they might signify the quarrying of stone. There is also a 'Stone Pit Field' south of Lowerfold; all the necessary building stone would undoubtedly be quarried locally. The large common area to the north is still noted, presumably for the use of tenants and freeholders.

The Knowles', one of the leading families in Quarlton, were first recorded in Edgworth and their first residence in Quarlton was by Richard Knowles, who was buried in the

Bolton Parish Church on 14th September 1590 and Alexander Knowles, buried there on 7th September 1619. Only the influential or wealthy were buried in the interior of the church rather than the grave-yard. Richard, son of the above Richard, was at Top of Quarlton in the 1620 plan, whilst the Thomas Knowles, at Lowerfold in 1620, was probably Richard's cousin. Members of the Knowles' family farmed at Top of Quarlton, Lowerfold, Maken Tower, Longshaw Head, Wickenlow and at Hawkshaw Farm at various times up to the mid-1800s, as well as working as drovers and chapmen.

There are a few Wills of the Knowles family that give an insight to their standing in the 1700s. John Knowles of Quarlton who died 9th May, 1727 left an estate worth £65-11s-6d, including hay, plough and irons but only one horse and two beasts. His furniture suggests a high level of comfort for the time and even included a clock. As he left £70 to each of his sons in law, James Orrell of Edgworth and James Wood of Turton, to satisfy marriage contracts, it rather looks as if those bequests were settled before the appraisal. We do not know where John lived but his goods suggest one of the larger farms.

Another Will dated 10th November 1765, is that of Mary Knowles, widow of Thomas Knowles, late of Quarlton, who had been a chapman: they were the traders or merchants who bought and sold yarn and woven cloth from the domestic workplace to sell in the markets of Bolton and Manchester. They had the lease of Maken Tower (Moor Bottom Road) from William Wright; son John Knowles was amongst family beneficiaries.

The Knowles family emerge as the entrepreneurs of the area and by this time are well established farmers or chapmen. An interesting marriage registration at Bolton Parish Church details James Knowles, who married Elizabeth Haslam of Harwood on 17th May 1740, and is described as a drover or chapman. He was buried at Turton, 11th June 1779.

Quarlton residents having no Chapel of Ease used the Parish Church of Bolton for baptism, marriage and burial, although Turton was used for burials from the mid-1700s. Some marriages and baptisms were also officiated at Bradshaw and Turton Chapel as on November 20th 1664, when the marriage of Peter Bromiley of Turton and Ann Butler of Quarlton was officiated at Bradshaw Chapel by Robert Harpur, the then Vicar of Bolton. Some baptisms and marriages were also solemnised at Holcombe Chapel.

Although the Knowles' lived at Top of Quarlton during this period, in common with other Quarlton messuages, there were two separate farmsteads. The second one here was probably linked to the barn at the north-east of the main building. On top of the wall adjacent to this barn is a carved date of 1629.

William Wright's Quarlton Estate Plan of 1727.

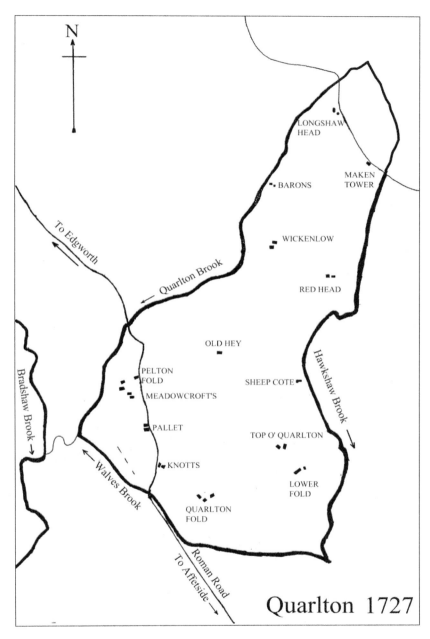

Quarlton Farms marked on William Wright's Map of 1727.

Barons Farmhouse
and barn 1940.

Meadowcrofts Farmhouse
1975.

Meadowcrofts
Farmhouse: living
room with fireplace
bressummer and
'heck', 1999.

Longshawhead Barn adjacent to Moor Bottom Road leading round to Holcombe.

Red Earth Farm and Barn 1977.

Red Earth, after rebuild in 1996.

In the early 1700s this farm was tenanted by the Longworth family from Entwistle. Thomas Longworth died at Quarlton on 11th March, 1759 and was buried at Turton leaving an outstanding lease of 14 years to run on his Top o' Quarlton farm. Son John continued to run the farm until 21st June 1773 when he hanged himself in his own barn at Top of Quarlton. The report in the 'Manchester Mercury' says he rose that day at 5 o'clock and was seen by his neighbour looking at his corn crop. The Coroner could not account for his death because John Longworth was *in good circumstances* and the suicide was put down to lunacy. It is felt within the present Longworth family that with the lease running out that year, requiring a substantial payment for renewal, John Longworth may have feared eviction if there was insufficient time for the corn to ripen and sell before the lease ran out. In the event, John's uncle, Ralph Longworth from nearby Redisher helped out the widow.

Wickenlow was another location which probably included two families in the 1700s shown from baptism records at Holcombe Chapel. In 1733 Robert, son of Richard Makin of 'Whickenlow' was baptised 10th February 1741, their daughter Betty was baptised 20th August of the same year, and early in 1742 James, son of Christopher Isherwood of 'Whickenlow' was also baptised. Another Holcombe Chapel baptism was that of Ellen, daughter of John Haslam of Maken Tower on 25th November 1739.

Mr Meadowcroft, who gave his name to Meadowcrofts, sold this property to Richard Orrell in the late 1700s who in his Will of 1799 left the house to his son Thomas. There were two date-stones, 1620 TMO, M signifying Meadowcroft. and 1745, ACD, possibly denoting Alexander Chadwick and his wife.

Of the other section of free land, Barons, we have more documentary evidence of change. Thomas Warburton of Stubbings, gent, sold the property to Lawrence Horrocks of Edgworth, yeoman, on the 24th May 1649, when it was described as late in the tenure of William Baron of Quarlton: from then on this property was known as Barons. On 2nd April 1674, Lawrence Horrocks sold Barons to William Entwistle of Quarlton, husbandman. William died 3rd May 1727 bequeathing Barons to his grandson, John Entwistle of Quarlton. The Wright map of 1727 puts Barons down to Thomas Entwistle who was at this time executor of William's Will. Included with the executors is John Entwistle of Edgworth but late of Longshaw Head.

The day John Entwistle acquired Barons under his grandfather's Will, he sold it to Andrew Knowles of Edgworth, yeoman. On Andrew Knowles' death his executors sold Barons to John Bury of Quarlton, yeoman, on 3rd July 1746, who himself died on 4th January 1768 leaving his estate to his grandson George, subject to charges to his grand-daughter Ann.

A contemporary document describes Barons as *'consisting of two cottages or dwelling houses, one barn, one shippon and enclosures called Field above the house, the Clough, the Furthermost Field, Further Meadow, Meadow under the House and Meadow at the Clough, in all 4 acres'* (8.6 statute acres).

On 2nd June 1777 Barons ownership was confirmed to Henry Entwistle of Edgworth, yeoman and Ann his wife, grand-daughter of John Bury.

Barons Farm (upper) and Barons Barn (lower).

Chapter IV ENCLOSURE AND TURNPIKE

In a previous chapter we have outlined the Quarlton rights of common on Edgworth Moor. The freeholders of all three townships, Edgworth, Entwistle and Quarlton, petitioned Parliament for enclosure of Edgworth Common and submitted *'that the moor in its present state offered little benefit and might be considerably improved and rendered of great value to the owners and to the public if the moor was enclosed'*. An act was finally approved in 1795 to enable the *'dividing, allotting and enclosing of a certain tract of Common called Edgworth Moor containing four hundred acres of customary measure (8 yards to the rod) or thereabouts upon which the Owners of Estates in the Townships Edgworth, Entwistle and Quarlton in the Parish of Bolton have Rights of Common'*.

The Commissioners appointed were Thomas Eccles of Lower Darwen, Ralph Fletcher of Haulgh and James Brandwood of Edgworth; Ralph Fletcher was also appointed Surveyor. The first meeting of the Commissioners was called for 18th June 1795 at the House of John Rostron, known by the sign of the White Horse (this was the old White Horse near Walleach) in Edgworth.

Possibly because of the small allotment - 54 acres total - with few roads to be set-out, etc, Quarlton owners of land were not called to contribute to the overall expense of the Act, providing they fenced off their allotment from other parts of the Common by 29th September 1796. They were not however, allowed plots for turbary as were the other 46 freeholders of Edgworth and Entwistle who were allotted turbary strips on Crowthorn Hill.

The Commissioners were responsible for establishing an improved road system and a series of new roads were built including Mill Highway (Bolton Road), Crowthorn Highway connecting up with Moor Bottom Road and Lumsgate Highway (Plantation Road) which connected at Lumsgate with the lanes running to Red Head, Clough Bottom (on the border of Hawkshaw) and the top of Old Ben Lane, running through Old Heys and down to Bury Road at the top of Knotts Brow.

On the Enclosure Map of 1796, Lumsgate Highway, at the Quarlton boundary ie Lumsgate (the 1850 OS Map notes Lum Well at this point) there is a note which reads *'New Road (vide bond given by landowners of Quarlton)'* as well as *'Road leading to Ben Lane and to Bolton'*. This note of *'New Road'* refers to a proposed road through Quarlton to join the proposed Turnpike Road near Brick Kiln as described on the Little Bolton to Edenfield Turnpike Trust Plan of 1797.

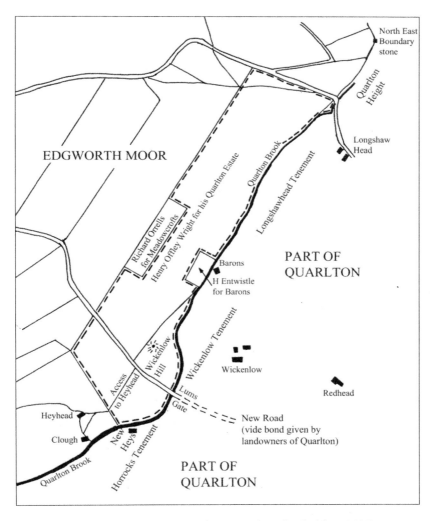

Edgworth Enclosure Awards to Quarlton freeholders 1797.

The Enclosure Awards were thus:

Award No	Freeholder	Qualifying Propery	Moor			Turbary
			A	R	P	
1 (A,B,C,D)	Henry Offley Wright	Quarlton Estate	49	3	8	-
2	Henry Entwistle	Barons	0	3	16	-
3	Richard Orrell	Meadowcrofts	3	1	16	-
Total Allotment to Quarlton Freeholders			54	0	0	

Rev Henry Offley Wright's allotment of 49a.3r.8p in Edgworth Township ran from the Crowthorn Highway in the north, southwards roughly parallel to Quarlton Brook to just south of the new Lumsgate Highway (Plantation Road). Rev Wright was able to establish two new farms; the area south of Lumsgate Highway with 18.694 acres was formed into Sandy Bank Farm - there being *'Sand Hole'* marked on the Enclosure Map. The northerly part of the Wright's Award formed the new Wickenlow Hill Farm.

The Henry Entwistle award for Barons was a small area adjacent but over the Quarlton Brook; an access road was allowed through Wickenlow Hill Farm land. The Orrell award for Meadowcrofts was a rectangular section to the west of the Wright award.

The new Lumsgate Highway (Plantation Road) allowed access through Sandy Bank Farm land to Clough and Heyhead Farms in Edgworth to the west of Quarlton Brook, as well as improved easterly access to Wickenlow, New Heys and Red Head Farms, and joining up with Old Ben Lane.

The Awards benefited the three freeholders greatly and Quarlton Township as a whole, particularly the northern farms with the much improved access road of Lumsgate Highway. Crowthorn Highway in the north benefited Longshaw Head and Maken Tower Farms.

The Turnpike Act directly affecting Quarlton was the Act of 19th June 1797 *'for amending, widening, altering and Keeping in Repair the road from or from near Edenfield Chapel in the Township of Tottington Higher End in the Parish of Bury to the Township of Little Bolton in le Moors'*. The Act also included a new road from Booth Pits to Bury Bridge.

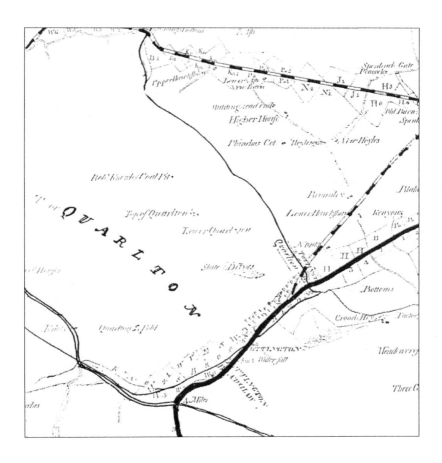

Section of the Little Bolton to Edenfield Turnpike Road passing through the south-eastern corner of Quarlton. The turnpike road is shown by a wide, solid black line. Similar broken lines show routes of proposed roads that were never built.

This Turnpike trust was presented to Parliament by a large number of Bolton, Turton and Bury dignitaries who were willing to subscribe to the costs (as an investment) and to be trustees. The qualification necessary was that potential trustees must have an estate worth £100 per annum or a personal estate of £1000. Most of the trustee/subscribers had an interest in the Turnpike being manufacturers, landowners, quarry or mine operators or larger farmers of the district. Such was the advantage to some townships that they became corporate subscribers, ie Tonge, Edenfield and Turton.

Amongst potential trustee/subscribers noted in the Act were Andrew Knowles, Richard Orrell, John Ramsbottom and Rev Henry Offley Wright, all having interests in Quarlton. Subscriptions were called in as required for construction and in 1808 Andrew Knowles had subscribed £100 which with £47-3s-7d dividends accrued gave his total investment at that time as £147-3s-7d.

The first meeting of the Trust was held at the House of Mr William Scowcroft at Bradshaw Chapel, 'The Three Jolly Crofters', on 21st July 1797 when the first Trustees were sworn in including Andrew Knowles of Quarlton. At a meeting held on 4th May 1797, Ralph Fletcher was asked to set out the best line of road from Bradshaw Chapel following the Parliamentary line as nearly as possible and to be advertised to contractors for tender, providing that Mr Wright gave his land for the road in Bradshaw and Quarlton.

On 20th September 1797, Lawrence Shaw of Bury, an Attorney at Law, was appointed Clerk to the Trust, Ralph Fletcher of Bolton, Esq, was appointed Treasurer and Andrew Knowles of Quarlton, yeoman was appointed the Surveyor at a salary of three guineas per lunar month. Mr Andrew Knowles the Surveyor and Mr James Brandwood of Edgworth (the Steward of Turton Tower Estate) were ordered to immediately value the land on the line of the road and negotiate with the landowners.

The road was to be 12 yards wide, of which the centre 4 yards would be stone or gravel of 18 inches thickness graded to 12 inches thick on the edges. The stone and gravel could be taken from sources local to the road. On 7th Feb 1798, Mr John Mason was asked to survey the land lying between Quarlton Delf and the Turnpike Road near Quarlton Brook and report to the next meeting on the justification of building a road for the carting of materials from the Delf. There is no record that this road was built, but it could well have formed the Quarlton Coal Pit Lane in existence today – the stone delph being adjacent to the colliery site.

At a meeting of Trustees held at Thomas Cooper's 'Hare and Hounds' at Bury on 18th

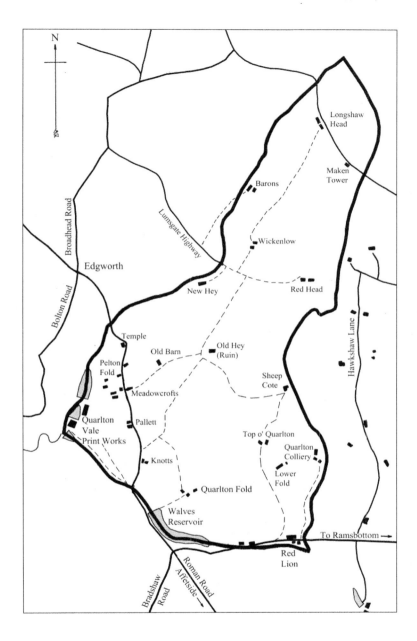

Map of Quarlton 1850, showing lanes (solid lines) and occupation roads (broken lines) with the print works, colliery and developments along the turnpike road.

October, 1798 and chaired by Robert Peel Esq, it was decided to appoint Robert Meadowcroft, yeoman of Woolfold, Bury as the Trust Surveyor in place of Andrew Knowles (who now declined the office).

It would appear that large sections of the road were completed by 13th March 1799 when a Committee was appointed to inspect the road and approve payment. Toll gates were agreed to be erected at Tonge Moor Gate and Booth Pits (the Bury branch road via Brandlesholme). The main section seemed to be operable by the end of 1799 as reports of toll gate rents as well as some abuse were made. Travel within Quarlton would be little changed but journeys into Bolton, Ramsbottom or Bury would have been easier. Because of traffic going to Bury via Affetside and Tottington (and avoiding toll charges), it was agreed in July 1800 that a Toll House and Bar be erected at the crossing of Affetside Lane (Watling Street).

The section of turnpike road from the Bull's Head to Hawkshaw passed through open country allowing development of property along its length. The first recorded is a plot of land leased in 1804 for the 'Red Lion Inn' and associated cottages. The Trustees of the Turnpike Trust held one of their meetings at the House of John Top, the 'Red Lion' in Quarlton on 3rd July 1806.

The Turnpike Trust Plan shows two roads crossing Quarlton that were never built. A branch road was proposed to run from near Lowe Farm south of Spenleach to Clough Bottom across the Hawkshaw Brook and running south of Red Head and Wickenlow to join the newly made Lumsgate Highway formed from the Enclosure of Edgworth Moor. The second proposed branch ran from the turnpike road some 400 yards west of the Quarlton Brook bridge and across to Spenleach and Redisher. The initial line of this new road is now the entrance road to Lower Fold and Top of Quarlton.

There was little further to report on the Quarlton section of the new road apart from periodic complaints to the Township Surveyor that road repairs were not satisfactory. However, in June 1810, it was ordered that the watering trough in Quarlton be removed to Nuttall Lane (nearer Ramsbottom). The 'Accounts of Subscribers' in January 1813 showed that Andrew Knowles' total was £183-19s-3d and Rev H O Wright's was £266-13s-6d in a total subscription of £10,308-16s-8d.

The Act of 1797 was followed by a similar Act of 8th April 1830 to confirm the Edenfield Chapel to Little Bolton road and the Booth Pits to Bury Bridge road with additional branches, including a new road from near the Bull's Head junction with Watling Street to Tottington and Bury Bridge - the new Turton Road leading to Tottington. It was also planned to improve the standard of road from the Bull's Head to Four Lane Ends, Edgworth.

Chapter V   QUARLTON COLLIERY

The story of Quarlton Colliery concerns a branch of the Knowles' family who initially prospered as yeomen farmers at Top of Quarlton Farm, but soon started mining around their property. Starting with perhaps twenty colliers at Quarlton, they finally developed into one of the largest colliery companies in Lancashire.

Richard Knowles appears to be the first of the family to farm in Quarlton and his father John (of Edgworth), who died in 1582, was probably the first of the Knowles in the Turton district. Richard Knowles, buried in Bolton Parish Church on September 14th 1590, left his Quarlton estate (Top of Quarlton) to his son Richard who died about 1650. This Richard Knowles is recorded on Barton's 1620 map as tenant of Top of Quarlton. He in turn was succeeded by another Richard, who dying young, was buried at Bolton on May 26th 1638. The heir, another Robert Knowles, was born in 1630 and buried at Turton Chapel on November 19th 1701. He restored the main part of the farmhouse and ornamented his fireplace with an elaborate plaster decoration bearing the intitials of Robert, his wife Ann (Warburton) and the date 1670.

The plaster panel was eventually removed by Sir Lees Knowles for incorporation into his house at Pendlebury. He later acquired Turton Tower in 1903 and on his death in 1930 his widow, Lady Nina Knowles, presented in his memory, the Tower and grounds to the Turton Urban District Council. It is said that the plaster panel, unfortunately damaged, was later given to Turton Tower Museum for safe-keeping although its current whereabouts is unknown.

The first Richard Knowles to settle in Quarlton had a brother Alexander who began farming Lower Fold, Quarlton and was probably the direct ancestor of Thomas Knowles, tenant of Lower Fold in the 1620 Barton map and originator of the datestone lettered '1627 TKIBM'.

Robert Knowles (1630-1701) with his son Andrew (1659-1730) would have undertaken the early mining of coal on the Quarlton property. Andrew's son, Robert (1710-1780) became wealthy enough to move to Little Bolton where he built 'Eagley Bank', although his son, Andrew (1736-1810) remained at Quarlton, probably concentrating on coal mining there rather than farming. He was the last of this branch of the Knowles family to live in Quarlton.

Although no longer existing, there was a datestone of 1754 RKJ on Eagley Bank that was moved when the house was extended at the rear in 1864. It is thought that the house was built by Robert Knowles and his wife Jane (Kinder of Breightmet Hall) in 1754. It appears that although living at Eagley Bank, the family still retained the tenancy of Top of Quarlton farm, probably for the coal mining rights. It is also likely that Andrew's mining experience equipped him to become the Turnpike Trust Surveyor in 1795. Andrew's son Robert Knowles (1755 to 1819) continued to live at Eagley Bank with seven sons and five daughters, the eldest of whom, Andrew, born April 16th, 1783, was to become one of the largest colliery proprietors of his time.

Pigot's Directory of Lancashire, 1822, records Andrew Knowles of Little Bolton as a Coal Owner/Merchant suggesting that his mining interests were extending beyond Quarlton, while the Little Bolton address refers to Eagley Bank which was in the Township of Little Bolton. The Land Tax return of 1825 refers to the Quarlton Coal Pit occupied by Andrew Knowles. Pigot and Dean's Directory of Bolton of 1836 and 1843 notes Andrew Knowles as being a Coal Owner and Merchant operating from Church Wharf, Bolton (terminus of the Manchester, Bolton and Bury Canal) and living at Eagley Bank.

By admission into partnership of Andrew's four sons, Robert, Thomas, John and James, the concern became Andrew Knowles and Sons in 1839. At this time the company had mining interests in Radcliffe, Little Lever, Little Bolton, Darcy Lever, Kearsley, Clifton and Pendlebury, including Clifton Hall and Agecroft Collieries. Andrew Knowles and Sons remained a private family firm until incorporated into a public limited company in 1873.

Andrew Knowles retained his family ties with the Quarlton area by having his sons baptised at Turton (Thomas, John and James) and Walmsley (Robert) Chapels and Eagley Bank House was only just over the Eagley Brook, from Turton Township. At the same time Andrew played a part in Bolton's industrial and municipal growth by being elected a Councillor for the East Ward of the new Borough of Bolton in December, 1838. It is suggested that Andrew Lane is named after Andrew Knowles who was a much respected resident of the area.

Andrew Knowles died on December 8th 1847 and was buried at Turton. Andrew's four sons continued to operate the company. Robert lived at Swinton Old Hall, Thomas at Clevely Bank, Pendlebury, John at Darcy Lever and James at Eagley Bank. It seems that each brother took charge of different collieries as detailed in Mackies Bolton Directory of 1849. Andrew Knowles and Sons still had an office at Canal Wharf 'Mr John' was at Little Lever, 'Mr James' at Astley Bank and no doubt Robert and Thomas were concerned with the collieries near their homes.

The little coalfield at Quarlton is based on the Upper Mountain Mine that outcrops on the west side of Top of Quarlton and Lower Fold farmsteads and extends to the north until it is cut out by a fault near Old Heys Farm. In the other direction it descends the hill to intersect the main road on the west side of Walves Cottages. From the outcrop, the two feet thick seam inclines steeply to the east at angles of up

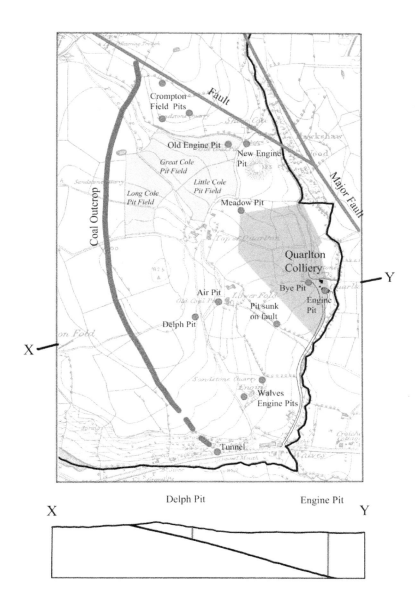

Mining activities in the Upper Mountain Mine at Quarlton superimposed on the 6 inch OS Map of 1850. The last area to be worked is shaded grey. Fields containing mining activities in 1727 are shaded pink. Section XY shows the inclination and depth of the coal seam across the area.

to 20° and reaches a depth of about 500 feet at the township boundary with Hawkshaw. The seam extends into Hawkshaw for a short distance before being cut out by a very large north-south fault.

The first documentary evidence of mining is provided by the Quarlton Estate plan of 1727 on which three of the field names record the presence of coal pits; 'Great Cole Pit Field', 'Little Cole Pit Field' and 'Long Cole Pit Field'. They are located between Top of Quarlton and Sheep Cote farmsteads and extend westwards towards the outcrop of the seam (see map). There is no evidence of mining on the earlier estate plan of 1620 and it can be assumed that extraction in Quarlton, as in many other places in the Bolton area, began sometime after the middle of the seventeenth century.

The seam would have been discovered somewhere along the outcrop where there is little cover of superficial material. Initially mining would have been confined to an area roughly on the west side of Top of Quarlton, where the coal was at fairly shallow depth and drainage by gravity into a nearby valley could be arranged by means of a tunnel In such areas of shallow mining it was usual to provide shafts at fairly frequent intervals to improve ventilation and enable the coal to be brought easily to the surface without the need for extensive haulage underground. The landowner would usually require the shafts to be filled as mining progressed to preserve the agricultural value of the land. However as mining reached deeper levels, shaft sinking would become progressively more expensive necessitating a much reduced number of shafts, improved ventilating techniques and better underground haulage.

Further documentary evidence of mining is provided by a plan of the new turnpike road made around 1797 which shows a single coal pit owned by Mr Andrew Knowles on the north side of Top of Quarlton near Sheep Cote in a position that seems to coincide with a shaft called 'Old Engine Pit' on later plans.

Finally there is a plan of the deepest workings under Lawrence Wright's estate made in 1857, which shows the position of panels of coal being worked after 1841, together with several shafts in adjacent old workings and some connecting roadways. At that time the two working shafts were close to the Hawkshaw boundary at a site called 'Quarlton Colliery' on the 6 inch OS map. Coincidentally there is also an estate plan of 1857 which shows the surface arrangements of Quarlton Colliery and the access road alongside Hawkshaw Brook that provided an outlet to the turnpike opposite the Red Lion at Walves.

A copy of an 1834 lease has survived between Andrew Knowles of Little Bolton and Lawrence Wright which allows Knowles to mine coal on Wright's estates in Quarlton and Bradshaw. The lease was for 16 years at a rent of £400 per year plus

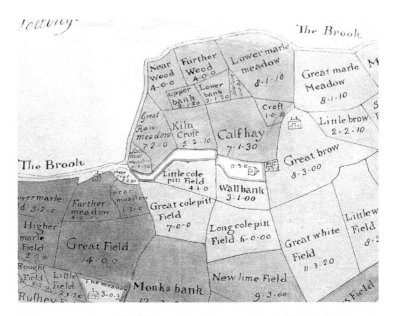

Part of the estate plan of 1727 showing 'Great cole pitt Field', 'Little cole pitt Field' and 'Long cole pitt Field'.

Site of the main pit head for Quarlton Colliery.

one fifth of the coal sales revenue. It concerned *'all mines, beds, delphs and veins of coal, cannel smut and slack open and to be found in Bradshaw and Quarlton'*. Under its terms Knowles was fairly free to carry out mining operation as he wished providing that he reinstated the land before the lease expired,. He could *'open any roads, pits, shafts, drains, soughs, adits, tunnels and culverts of water or erect or take down any whimseys or other engines, stables, cabins, huts, and ovens'*. Also he could use *'any stream, rivulet or culvert for working steam engines or water wheels'* and was free to make bricks from clay and get stone. But he was to keep proper accounts and plans and otherwise work the seam systematically. The terms seem to have been observed insofar as there is now no trace of the original shafts. It may be noted that the lease was quite exacting and revenues due to the landowner seem very substantial. That Knowles should agree to such a lease is probably a reflection of the value of the seam.

The 1857 mine plan made to show workings under Lawrence's land provides the most detailed record of the way mining progressed. The workings are shown in greatest detail around the area then being worked, which was called 'Quarlton Colliery', but the location of other shafts in the old working are recorded. The plan is remarkable for the large number of shafts called 'Engine Pit'. There are two 'Walves Engine Pits', an 'Old Engine Pit' and 'New Engine Pit' close together near Sheep Cote and yet another 'Engine Pit' at the main 'Quarlton Colliery' site. The name usually implies that the pit was used for pumping and suggests that mining and associated drainage activities were carried out at two separate locations (Walves and Sheep Cote) in earlier years before moving to 'Quarlton Colliery' for the final and deepest workings.

In addition the mine plan records an 'Air Pit' at Lower Houses, on the hillside above 'Quarlton Colliery' at a spot where the altitude would provide for a current of air through the workings. The tunnel at Walves is not specifically recorded on the mine plan and presumably was connected with an earlier stage of working. From its position and elevation it appears to give level access to workings around the base of Delph Pit.

There is also a second tunnel mouth above the Lodge End Cottage on Ramsbottom Road which could be a working drift or a drainage sough. An estate map of 1857 suggests this was a drift mine working a coal seam 13-18 inches thick at a lower level than the Upper Mountain Mine of Quarlton Colliery.

Over the years the colliery was not without its grim list of accidents. Coal mining was always hazardous and Quarlton Colliery was no exception. A burial registered at Holcombe Chapel on 14th February 1800 was of John Hargreaves aged 26 who was killed at Top of Quarlton Coal Pit.

A Bolton newspaper reports on 31st January 1846: '*An inquest was held Tuesday last at the Red Lion Inn, Quarlton before E Molesworth, Deputy Coroner on the body of a boy aged 8 years named Ralph, son of John Scholes of Tottington. It appeared that the deceased along with some other men were engaged in getting coal in a pit owned by A Knowles and Sons at Quarlton on 23rd instant when one of the men struck his pick through into an old coalmine adjoining the one in which they were working which was full of water and before they could ascend the shaft the boy was overpowered by the water and drowned* - Verdict, '*Accidental Death*'.

A tragedy at anytime, but worsened by the fact that four years earlier the Coal Mines Act of 1842 had made it illegal to employ females and boys under 10 years of age underground after March, 1843. The Coroner either ignored this Act or was ignorant of the ruling; quite a reflection on the Knowles' company

The Bolton Chronicle of 5 February 1853 reported: '*On Saturday last, Martin Harris an overlooker was killed while at work at a coal pit belonging to Messers Knowles at Quarlton. It appears he descended a portion of the shaft in order to attach a clack* [valve] *to a pump, and for some purpose had communication by chain with the top of the shaft. The chain was partly wound upon a capstan, of which a person was placed in charge but in consequence of the handle being insecure, the whole chain unwound itself and dropped into the tub in which were Harris and a man named John Horrocks. Harris was thrown out of the tub and fell to the bottom of the pit, a distance of 70 yards (the entire depth being 180 yards) the underlooker being killed by the fall; Horrocks was not seriously injured*'. The only shaft used for pumping at this date would be the 'Engine Shaft' at the main colliery site which was the deepest at Quarlton and exceptionally deep for a shaft in Turton.

Included in the Coal Mine Acts of 1842 was a requirement to appoint Mines Inspectors to enforce the Act and Mr Joseph Dickinson was appointed as Inspector for the whole of the North-West covering an area bounded by and including North Wales, Oldham and Burnley up to Barrow. In his reports beginning in 1854 he lists 43 collieries in the Bolton area. Andrew Knowles and Sons owned Hacken, Little Lever; Little Bolton; Quarlton, Top o' th' Lane, Darcy Lever and Turton Moor collieries. They also owned in the Manchester area Agecroft, Pendlebury; Clifton Hall, Clifton Moss and Pendleton collieries. In Mr Dickinson's systematic lists of working collieries 'Quarlton Colliery' belonging to 'A Knowles' appeared each year until 1860 after which there were no entries, presumably because the colliery had closed. Finally after period of 200 years, the Quarlton pits had become exhausted. The shafts would be filled or otherwise made secure, the workings abandoned, the colliers would find work elsewhere and the equipment would be disposed of.

A Bolton Newspaper on 9th February 1861 advertised the following sale:- *'Colliery Plant to be sold by private treaty at Quarlton Colliery. The whole of the plant now working consisting of a double acting pumping engine 6 foot stroke and 33 inches in diameter. Three brass working barrels, 18 inches, 13 inches and 12 inches diameter. Pump rods, buckets, clacks and 100 yards of pump trees. One 10 horse power condensing winding engine, spur wheels and rope drum. One 6 horse power horizontal engine. Four cylindrical steam boilers of various sizes and fixings. Headgear, pulley and rope. One double power capstan, pulleys and chain. One 5 ton weighing machine and other articles. The whole in good working order and will be ready for removal in one month. Apply. Mr James Knowles, Eagley Bank, Nr Bolton'.*

The plant described covers the requirements of the final stages of Quarlton Colliery with a pumping pit near the Hawkshaw Brook and a winding shaft for both men and coal a little higher up the slope. The steam beam engine of 6 foot stroke drew up the water through a brass barrel by the pump rods which would have been moved up and down by the timber pump trees, similar to the old style hand operated water pump but in this case drawing up about 30 cubic feet of water per stroke from an underground lodge up to an outlet tunnel running into the Hawkshaw Brook.

The steam winding engine would at this time also be a beam engine with gearing from the flywheel to the winding drum, winding the rope (probably of flat rectangular section) over the headgear wheel and pulling up either a 'cage', 'tubs', or simple 'basket'.

The 6 horse power horizontal engine would, through the capstan and pulleys, be used for haulage of wagons underground. The weighbridge would be of the platform type to weigh off loads of coal to the customer - quite likely the Two Brooks Bleach Works and other local mills.

The census records confirm the closing date of the colliery. The 1841 Census shows coalminers living at Top of Quarlton, James Hamer (40), at Knotts, John Fletcher (40) and John Fletcher (15). Thirteen others lived at the Walves Cottages, Thomas Vickers (35), John Isherwood (40), Thomas Holt (16), James Holt (12), John Walsh (35), Thomas Booth (20), John Nuttall (30), Thomas Isherwood (14), John Kay (15), Squire Smith (30), Isaac Orrell (25) and James Smith (25). In 1851 there were 21 coal miners living in the Walves Cottages, 10 in 1861 and only one in 1871, William Isherwood (39). The old colliery site can now only be found by the study of a map, but the old Coal Pit Lane remains from the Red Lion as a delightful footpath.

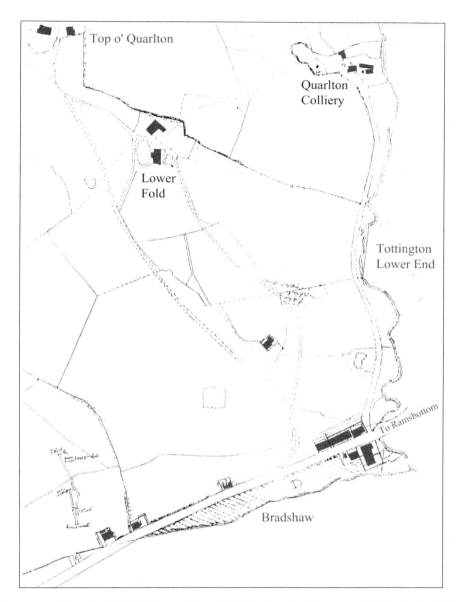

An extract from the Wright Estate Map of 1857, showing Quarlton Colliery in its final stage on Coal Pit Lane. The lanes to Top of Quarlton and Lower Fold are shown as well as an old lane to an earlier pit above Delph Cottages. Details of an old coal tunnel are included on the lower left of the plan.

Chapter VI   QUARLTON VALE PRINTWORKS

Quarlton Vale is the descriptive name of the steep sided valley straddling the Quarlton (or Walleach) Brook in the lower reaches of the valley at the junction of the boundaries of Edgworth, Quarlton and Bradshaw Townships marked by the confluence of the Quarlton Brook with the Walves Brook.

Our earliest documentary evidence on this area is from an Indenture of 1804 when on 13th October, William Woodcock, described as a *'Gentleman of Holcombe'*, leased for 999 years a plot of land to John Hall, a cotton spinner of Great Bolton, at an annual rent of £15-3s-1d. This plot in Edgworth being part of a field known as Potato Holme of the Hillock Farm was on the Quarlton Brook and abutted up to a similar plot in Quarlton lately leased to John Hall by Richard Orrell of Quarlton, a yeoman. John Hall also had the right to impound and divert the brook with a weir or dam to form a reservoir *'no more than 10 feet higher than the old weir thereunto erected'*. A small sketch plan detailed *'an old stone mill in ruins'* and appeared to be in the part of the valley now covered by Quarlton Print Works Reservoir. The earlier Indenture of 23rd May 1804 for land on the Quarlton side reserved to Isaac Orrell and his heirs a right of road to the reservoir and the right to fish.

Higher up the valley on the Edgworth side of the brook, where Barlow Park was later developed, was a small mill used initially as a cotton mill but in the early 1800s as a calico printing works run by a partnership called Spencer, Gee and Company. This was in a locality called Russia and on the 1850 OS Map designated Higher Russia. William Kingsley, a noted Edgworth local historian of the 1930s records that Spencer, Gee and Company also had block printers working on the top floor of the 'White Horse' (built 1810).

This partnership of Spencer, Gee and Company was made up of William Spencer, John Gee, Richard Boardman, John Fairclough, John Bilsborrow, Richard Thornborrow, John Starkie, George Scholes, James Smith and Thomas Brierly. On 11th July 1815, Richard Boardman, late of Edgworth, gave notice in the Manchester Mercury to withdraw from the Partnership then trading as Calico Printers at Russia in the Township of Edgworth.

William Spencer was born at Bury in 1784, being the son of James and Jane Spencer (calico printer and colour mixer) and was the managing partner living at the adjacent Brandwood Fold. It is thought, after the changes noted above in 1815, that he moved down the valley and started to develop Quarlton Vale Printworks - the first date-stone being 1825 - as Spencer, Smith and Fairclough. James Smith lived at Pallet starting a connection with Quarlton Vale Works that lasted for the next 100 years.

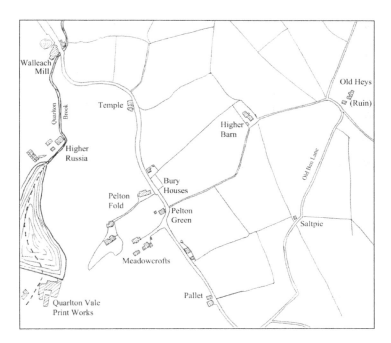

South-west Quarlton in 1850. Walleach 'Engine Mill' and Higher Russia Print Works are on Quarlton Brook above Quarlton Vale Print Works. Bury Road goes round Temple Farm before it was straightened in 1958.

Saltpie Cottage property built adjacent to Old Ben Lane c1825.

Part of Quarlton Vale Works that may have developed separately to the main works is the 'Holm Shop', which is on a small plot of land, part in Quarlton and part in Bradshaw, on the south-western tip of Quarlton. It used a reservoir at the rear on Birches land fed from Walves Reservoir by pipeline. Unfortunately there is no early record, but Walves Reservoir was built in the early 1800s and is on Greenwood's Map of 1818. The 'Holm Shop' was the last building to be demolished in 1996 and could well have housed the block printers moved from the 'White Horse' by Spencer, Gee and Company in 1815.

William Spencer died on the 26th May 1826 and his wife Mary (Livesey) and family moved to Belmont where sons William, Thomas, James and Joseph occupied Belmont Printworks. In 1839, William Spencer junior bought the Springside Paper Mill with the help of his father-in-law, Robert Orrell (who owned Ryecroft Mill in Belmont) and Charles Turner (Mr Orrell's chief clerk).

The remaining partners at Quarlton, Messrs Smith and Fairclough, continued to run the Quarlton Vale operation until on 13th May 1828 they advertised for auction what appears to be the Higher Russia concern:-

'A freehold estate situate at Brandwood Fold, Edgworth containing 20 statute acres of land with valuable Printworks thereon, now in the occupation of Messrs Smith and Fairclough, Calico Printers. The buildings consist of a farmhouse, out-buildings, a large new dwelling house, nine cottages, a small mill, a large new drying house, several reservoirs and many springs of excellent water, and a small stream runs through. The Estate is five miles from Bolton. There are coals within a quarter of a mile.'

It is interesting to note that the estate to be auctioned includes one of the two farms of Brandwood Fold, ie, farmhouse, buildings and cottages. The large new dwelling house could be Sandy Bank House which overlooked the Higher Russia site. The local coal pit was Andrew Knowles' Turton Bottom Colliery.

The Quarlton Vale Works continued downstream under the direction of Messrs Smith and Fairclough who unfortunately became bankrupt. Details of an auction to be held 6th October, 1831 at the Bridge Inn, Bolton-le-Moors. were published in the Bolton newspapers as follows:

Lot I   *The Printworks called Quarlton Vale situate in Edgworth and Quarlton. Includes the land on which the works are erected together with lodges, reservoir, streams of water and water-wheel. The machinery is modern and capable of employing more than 400 men. The buildings are in good repair. To be held for the balance of 999 years from 1804 at a rent of £18 pa.*

Lot II   *A small plot of land adjoining the Printworks with 5 cottages & stable in the occupation of John Fairbrother & others including the bankrupt.*

Lot III   *A plot of land at the Bottoms in Edgworth of 277 sq yds with cottage, wheelwright's shop & smithy now in the possession of Henry Worsley.*

Lot IV   *A plot of land 806 sq yds at the Bottoms in Edgworth and 15 cottages erected thereon, in the occupation of Robert Isherwood, John Becker and others.*

Lot V   *A plot of land situate at Wall Leach, Moorgate in Edgworth with 3 dwelling houses, stable & shippon etc, now in the occupation of John Fairclough & his son John, & Ellen Haslam.*

The leases on Lot II and III are for 999 years from 1804, Lot IV for 999 years from 1788 & Lot V 999 years from 1802. Abstract of Title, Plans etc, can be seen at the office of Mr Winder, Solicitor of Bolton-le-Moors or from Mr Giles Ashworth of Edgworth.

It would be reasonable to assume that the printworks were taken over by Robert Millington at this time because there was a date-stone *'1832-R M Senior'* and a later stone by his son *'1849-R M Junior'*. There seem to be some differences between the owners and operators as the Bolton directories quote in 1841, George and John Millington and in 1849 and 1853, George Millington.

However, on the first large scale Ordnance Survey Map surveyed 1844-47 the Quarlton Vale Print Works seem to be well developed with its own gasometer. The Millingtons have built Quarlton Vale House and as well as their access road from Bolton Road, Edgworth, also have an access road alongside the Walves Brook to the bottom of Knotts Brow - appropriately named Millington Lane.

A section of the works building and yard was built over the culverted stream and the entrance road and garden to Quarlton Vale House was also developed over the culvert. Having been developed from different pieces of land in Edgworth, Quarlton and Bradshaw, the final title was subject to six different ground rent leases dating from 1788 onwards.

The Millingtons, having met some financial difficulties, sold the whole Quarlton Vale Print Works to Robert Walker on 5th November 1858, the transaction being between George, John and William Milner Millington, James and Robert Knowles as one party and Robert Walker and Thomas Lever Rushton the other.

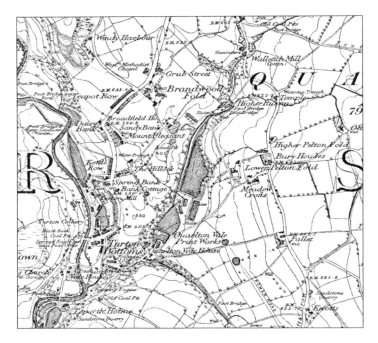

Quarlton Vale Print Works: 1850 OS Map.

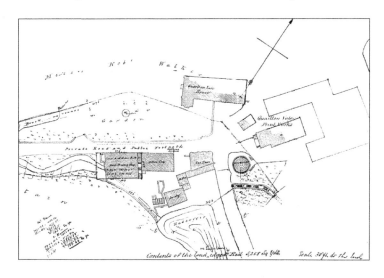

Quarlton Vale Print Works: plan of 1876.

48

Under Robert Walker, the works employed 224 people in 1861. In the 1874 Directory, James, George and Matthew Walker were noted as Calico Printers at Quarlton Vale as well as farmers at Pelton Fold, Pallet and Knotts. George Walker lived at Pallet. The 1876/7 Post Office Directory notes Robert Walker and Sons, Calico Printers at Quarlton Vale with Matthew Walker living at Vale House.

By 1881, Robert Walker & Sons are Calico Printers, Quarlton Vale and 66 Fountain Street Manchester. Both Matthew Walker and C E Walker live at Vale House, but the company of Walker Bros are now operating Spring Vale Mill (Bury Road, Edgworth) and the Old Engine Mill (alongside Quarlton Brook where it crosses Bury Road) and are described as manufacturers of *'plain and fancy goods'*.

The above descriptions applied with little variation through to the end of the century. In 1888, R Walker and Sons still operated Quarlton Vale as calico printers, Matthew Walker resided at Vale House, but Charles E Walker now lived at Mount Pleasant. By 1892, Charles had moved to Fir Trees, Turton with Matthew remaining at Vale House. The last directory reference to R Walker and Sons at Quarlton Vale was in 1902 by which time George and Matthew Walker had sold the Quarlton Vale Works to the Calico Printers' Association.

The calico printers formed a trading association in 1890 with an agreed schedule of trading following the pattern of the Bleachers' Association and in 1899 formed the Calico Printers' Association Ltd to amalgamate the companies. Forty six firms of printers, comprising 85% of the calico printing industry, joined the amalgamation. Within a serious decline in general business activity the Association had the facility to offer a comprehensive service to the world as well as central purchasing and technical development, and of course, standard selling prices.

It is not clear whether they continued to trade under the Walker name but on 25th January 1916 the Calico Printers' Association Ltd sold Quarlton Vale to Thomas Edward Clarke and his wife Mary Ann on condition that the premises and plant would not be used for calico printing, bleaching or finishing (other than yarn dyeing). The Clarkes lived at Harwood Lodge in Harwood and their business became that of yarn bleaching, employing about fifty people. Their three sons, 'Willy', Harry and Cyril later became involved in the management.

Thomas Edward Clarke died on 18th May, 1927 and Harold Porritt Clarke became senior director. Yarn bleaching continued up to and after World War II, suffering several periods of short time working. The whole textile industry was in a general decline against more overseas competition and, with yarn bleaching being a somewhat peripheral service, ran into financial difficulties leading eventually on 28th January

1964 to a decision to wind up the company voluntarily and appoint a liquidator to realise the assets.

The 1960s and 70s was a period when the Government wished to consolidate industrial resources into more competitive groupings and the IRC (Industrial Reorganisation Corporation) was set up to encourage, or in some cases force, mergers of like companies in order to reduce overall capacities, In the textile industry there were several schemes put forward to make it financially attractive for some companies to close up and scrap their plant. To this end the 'Yarn Processing Realisation Company Ltd' purchased the complete operation of Clarkes at Quarlton Vale on 24th March, 1965.

The buildings were used by small businesses for some years and gradually became derelict. The site was eventually sold to a developer with a longer term aim of housing development.

The reservoir had, since 1906, been used for fishing by the Longsight Anglers' Association founded in 1892 as a Prison Officers' Association from Belle Vue Prison in Longsight, Manchester. After the demolition of the prison, the society continued as a social club under the name of the Longsight Anglers' Association. Their original lease arrangement for fishing had been with the Calico Printers' Association and latterly with T E Clarke and Co. On the closure of Clarke's operation the Longsight Anglers' Association Trustees decided to purchase the reservoir from the Yarn Processing Realisation Co Ltd on 24th May, 1965.

The members of the Longsight Anglers' Association Trust continue to enjoy their sport having a vehicular and pedestrian right of way through the old works site to their land, being eleven acres in total with five acres of water. They have invested much time and money in securing the environmental attraction of this part of Quarlton valley.

The printworks site was eventually cleared by a developer and in 1990 the first of five houses erected. The residents jointly purchased the adjoining piece of land to the east including the old square stone chimney. After the chimney was repaired the surrounding land was planted up to form a woodland area.

Rober Walker
1794-1872.

Vale House,
Quarlton c1950.

Quarlton Vale
Print Works
reservoir 1997.

Quarlton Vale Print Works.

Main works building with feed reservoir at rear.

Works Office on the corner of Millington's Lane and Bury Road.

The old block printing shop, fed from the Walves reservoir.

Quarlton Vale Print Works.

Chapter VII THE NINETEENTH CENTURY

The building of the new Turnpike Road through Quarlton and the improvements to the Watling Street to Edgworth road encouraged and allowed cottage development for the housing of employees of the emerging industries of the district.

There had been associated cottages with the larger Quarlton farms for some time and the 1841 Census Returns indicate there were five families living at Top of Quarlton, four families at Quarlton Fold, two each at Pallet and Meadowcrofts. The return for Pelton Fold is most confusing, indicating eight families in 1841, reducing to five in 1851 and 1861. By 1871 and 1881 there were two families noted in each census, but strangely no farmer is noted for Pelton Fold in any of Census years 1841, 61, 71 and 81. It is felt that the land was farmed during the period in conjunction with the adjacent Meadowcrofts Farm and/or Temple Farm. These figures for Pelton Fold would include the main farmhouse at Lower Pelton Fold and the subsidiary building of Higher Pelton Fold on Bury Road.

Travelling from Edgworth over Quarlton Brook past Temple Farm, the first independent cottages we see on the left were originally built as a pair on a plot of land leased from the Wright's Estate on 25th March 1825 for a period of 999 years. This property was noted on an 1888 plan as Pelton Green but earlier as Bury Houses. The next group of five houses were built on a plot of land leased from the Wright's Estate on 1st December 1882, and the cottages carry the date-stone of '1884 AD West View Terrace'.

Opposite is a large detached house now called Pelton Green. The land on which it was built was leased for 999 years from the Wright Estate on 14th November 1805. A property was auctioned on June 14th 1865 at Cheetham's Farm, Chapeltown and described as *'The neat country residence known as Ivy Cottage, 4 beds, drawing room, sitting room, kitchen, scullery, wash-house, garden and yard situate at Pelton Green, Quarlton; occupied by Mr Handel Greenhalgh'*. The house was probably bought by Handel Greenhalgh. By 1881 it was occupied by Thomas Greenhalgh and his family.

On the north side of the road past Meadowcrofts Farm entrance lies a small terrace of cottages. Number 389 did carry the date 1847 but this has recently been removed. The land involved was originally part of Meadowcrofts Farm. It is not clear from documentary evidence who owned Meadowcrofts in the early 1800s after Richard Orrell's death in 1799, but an Indenture of 1897 refers to an earlier Indenture of 27th September 1847, when Isaac Orrell acquired the Meadowcroft Estate from James Cross, Thomas Lever Rushton and Robert Millington who may have been trustees acting for the Orrell family. This acquisition date by Isaac Orrell is noted on a date-stone on the Meadowcrofts barn, '1847 IOA', and may have influenced the use of the same date on No 389 Bury Road which could have been built by Isaac Orrell at this time on his land.

Isaac Orrell died on 16th February 1889 leaving Meadowcrofts Farm and land to his eldest son William Orrell and the cottages on Bury Road to his son Richard Orrell. At some time these cottages were extended into three, numbered 385, 387 and 389. The middle cottage, No 387, became the 'Farmers' Arms' public house. The 1871 Census details Richard Orrell, aged 40, as a 'beer seller' at the Farmers' Arms. The earlier 1861 Census reports Richard Orrell as an 'engine driver at print works' living in one of the cottages then called Mount Pleasant - probably later bequeathed to Richard Orrell. By 1881 William Entwistle is noted as the 'beer seller', while Richard Orrell had moved to live at Saltpie.

Saltpie was the only separate cottage development in Quarlton not on one of the main roads, the land was subject to a 999 year lease from Lawrence Wright to John Holt at an annual rental of £1-2s-6d for the 270 sq yard plot of land and dated 25th March 1825. This piece of land is described as being part of a close called the *'Lower Marled Earth'* and *'adjoining on the southerly side thereof to the old road leading from Lumsgate to Ben Lane End'*, and refers to that dwelling house now erected by John Holt. This field is noted on the 1727 Wright Map as Lower Marled Field and is adjacent to Old Ben Lane. The Census records for 1841 & 51 describe it as Marled Heath, adopting the name of Saltpie in 1861, by which time it houses two families.

The name of the road from Edgworth to Affetside has varied from Quarlton Road to Quarlton Lane and it was after the local Turnpike roads were built, particularly Turton Road to Tottington, that it was called Bury Road. One wonders whether this name goes back to 'Bury Houses' rather than the indirect route to Bury via Tottington?

Proceeding along Bury Road to the Bull's Head, the next property is Pallet Farm on the right, farmed in 1841 by Andrew Wadacker; it also housed the family of William Leigh, a block printer. After this time the land was farmed by adjacent farmers and in 1861 became the house of George Walker of Quarlton Vale Print Works who was also noted in the 1871 Census, and in 1881 when the house was designated Privet (Private) House and appeared at this time to have a rebuilt eastern front, making it a 'superior family house'.

The next property on the awkward corner leading down hill to the junction of the old Roman Road with Millington (Walker's or Clarke's) Lane is Knotts, one of the ancient farms marked on the Barton Map of 1620. By 1841 it is used as a cottage for John Fletcher and his family with no resident farmer and this applied right through to 1891 with Daniel Longworth, a farm labourer, and his family from1861 to 1891. It is likely

The pair of cottages on the access road to Temple Farm were built in 1825, while the row of four to the right rear carry a building date of 1884.

The detached cottage called Pelton Green was built c1805.

Originally built as two cottages, later as three, with the large recent extension to the front right. The centre cottage of the original three, No 387 was the 'Farmers' Arms' from c1860 to c1930.

Bury Road Cottages.

that Knotts' small acreage along with the Pallet land was farmed with Quarlton Fold land.

Alongside the road to the left is the Walves Reservoir covering the area of 8 acres.1r.13p built to supply water to the eastern side of the Quarlton Print Works. A pipe line ran from the embankment to the works alongside the stream and Millington Lane. The adjacent farm of Quarlton Fold had previously been served by an occupation road joining with Old Ben Lane to come down to the old road to Edgworth, Bolton, Turton or Affetside. With the building of the reservoir embankment across the valley a road was constructed from Quarlton Fold across the embankment to join the old road opposite the junction with Birches Road, a much more convenient access.

Quarlton Fold was a typical north Bolton fold in that it included more than one farmhouse and cottages - even on the 1727 Wright Estate Map it shows three buildings, all the others having one with the exception of Top of Quarlton with two.

The 1841 Census for Quarlton Fold included three farmers, Samuel Horrocks, Joshua Cookes and Alice Hamer, with Charles Dobson, a cotton weaver and family. It may be significant that William Horrocks, Thomas Scholes, Roger, Joseph and James Hamer and Mary Dobson were all designated cotton weavers at this period; these are all likely to be handloom weavers and possibly worked in their own domestic buildings. In 1851, John Brookes was noted as a farmer. James Wood, a labourer, and his family were in a separate residence with one house uninhabited. The date-stone of '1851 HW' on one of the Quarlton Fold barns probably marks a rebuild by Henry Wright. Only two families were noted in 1861, Riddel and Brooks and in 1871 Breckell and Farrington with James Ollerenshaw as farm bailiff. J Ollerenshaw was also a farmer in 1881. The farm bailiff description ties up with this interesting note made on 24th September, 1887 in the Scowcroft diaries; *'A carter for Thomas Glaister of Mill Hill Works was killed by being run over by the cart when going up to Quarlton Fold Farm with manure, Alfred Glaister being the occupier of the farm.'*

As already noted in the chapter on Quarlton Colliery, the Knowles' maintained their mining interest in the area around Top of Quarlton and Lower Fold but the farms themselves were tenanted separately for farming. This is indicated at the auction at the Bank Inn, Bolton on 11th July 1827 when Lot 2 was described as *'Top o' Quarlton during the life of John Mason (53 years) at present occupied as two farms in the occupation of Ellen Seddon and Samuel Greenhalgh, two dwelling houses, two cottages, outbuildings and 20 Cheshire acres, Sheepcote occupied by James Kay and Ellen Seddon, farmhouse, outbuildings and 9 Cheshire acres. Annual rent of £2-2s-0d. Mr Mason's life is insured in the sum of £700 in respect of these premises'*. This is an example of sub-letting and the first indication that Sheepcote Farm is being

Delph
Cottages
1977:
built c1849.

.

Lodge End, in the
foreground, was
originally built as two
cottages c1823, the row
of four cottages were
built c1850.

The 'Tunnel Garage'
So named by the
Taylor Brothers who
lived here and ran
their coach business.
There is a tunnel
mouth in the bank to
the rear.

absorbed into the Top of Quarlton holding, there being no census returns for Sheepcote as a separate farm.

In 1841, John Seddon (40) was the farmer at Top of Quarlton with his wife and family of seven. Christopher Dobson was also described as farming there with his family. In addition three other families were noted. As there was no 1841 reference to Lower Fold it is felt that Christopher Dobson was farming there rather than Top of Quarlton. John Seddon continued farming at Top of Quarlton in 1851 with two others, William Horrocks and Ann Hamer. John Seddon now 61 years old in 1861 was noted as farmer with 50 acres while three houses were noted as unoccupied as well as a cottage unoccupied at the coalpit. 1871 saw John Cottam farming there with 76 acres under the 'new' name of Quarlton Hall.

Below Top of Quarlton is Lower Fold Farm, which in 1841 was probably farmed by Christopher Dobson as noted above. By 1851 he had died and his widow Betty was farming Lower Fold with her sons Henry and Edward. Eldest son Leonard Dobson took over in 1861 with 50 acres, to be followed by John Aspinall farming 93 acres in 1871 when it was called Lower Fold House with George Knowles and family farming in 1881.

To the south of Lower Fold is a terrace of three cottages now known as Delph Cottages. An indenture dated 6th February 1849 between Rev Henry Wright and Betty Dobson, widow of Christopher Dobson, who was then farming at Lower Fold, leased two pieces of land in Quarlton for 999 years at £2-13s-4d per year. The first piece of 352 sq yds area is adjacent to the turnpike road and is probably the site of Nos 60-66 Ramsbottom Road opposite the Red Lion. The other plot of of 288 sq yds was surrounded by land owned by Rev Henry Wright and contained the dwelling houses erected by the late Christopher Dobson with access from the occupation road to Top of Quarlton. On 30th August 1875, John Knowles of Isherwood Fold, Edgworth, farmer, acting as trustee for the children of Christopher Dobson, sold the three Delph Cottages to William Bromiley of Harwood described as No 1 in occupation of Caroline Norris then Richard Mather, No 2 in occupation of William Isherwood then Thomas Entwistle, No 3 in occupation of Ann Isherwood.

Adjacent to these Delph Cottages on the 1850 OS Map is the word 'Engine'. The above indentures include no reference to colliery activities but we must assume the word is associated with the pit shafts near to the cottages.

The building of the turnpike road through Quarlton led to cottage development on both sides of the road, particularly at the entrance lane to Quarlton Colliery adjacent to the bridge. The earliest buildings were on a 1,100 sq yd plot of land defined by a deed

Walves Cottages opposite the Red Lion 1977.

Walves Cottages opposite the Red Lion 1999.

The entry to Coal Pit Lane adjacent to the bridge.

Walves Cottages.

dated 1st November 1804, on which the Red Lion was built. At first the inn incorporated four other cottages, only one of which is still in existence. A bowling green was established on the corner of the confluence of the Walves and Hawkshaw Brooks some time later and was in use regularly until the early 1930s. The same deed included a 240 sq yd plot on the opposite side of the new turnpike road. The early publicans of the Red Lion were John Top 1806; Thomas Bridge 1810; John Livesey 1815; John Cooper 1820; William Shaw 1841; Thomas Pilling 1851; William Greenhalgh 1861; Robert Urmston 1871; James Greenhalgh 1881 and 91.

The present corner terrace is built in ashlar stone and quite different to its immediate neighbours. An auction advertised to be held at the Bank Inn, Bolton on 23rd June, 1827, described Lot 5; *'Two cottages with stable and cowhouse adjoining, opposite the Red Lion public house in Quarlton. Occupiers, Peter Seddon, Peter Boardman and James Seddon'.*

On the 1850 OS Map this section nearest the brook is marked as a detached Smithy and Thomas Warden is included in the Census Returns as a blacksmith for the years 1841, 51, and 61. It has been suggested that this property was later a beer house or public house but we have no evidence. This group of three cottages were noted on a plan of 2nd September 1858 as being bought by Thomas Pilling from J & R Knowles. Thomas Pilling at this time was the landlord of the Red Lion. As the present building bears no resemblance to a smithy or small holding, the older structure could have been rebuilt into its present form after the demise of Thomas Warden, the blacksmith.

On the west side of the above mentioned three cottages is a pair of cottages set back to four more cottages set still further back. These were also bought by Thomas Pilling and are on a plot of land leased from Lawrence Wright on 4th December 1850, but the block of four have a much older appearance.

The four westerly cottages Nos 60, 62, 64 and 66 are the four cottages built on land leased from Rev Henry Wright by Betty Dobson (widow of Christopher Dobson) of Lower Fold Farm on 6th February 1849, and on a 1858 plan are occupied by Eliza Dobson, Leonard Dobson and John Knowles (married to a Miss Dobson).

Opposite these cottages alongside the Red Lion is a group of four houses, the land for which was leased from the Wright Estate on 1st March 1826. An 1869 plan shows the property as belonging to Miss Sarah Harrison who in the 1871 census is recorded as a school mistress living with her blind sister Elizabeth and two nephews. An extract from the book 'St Marys, Hawkshaw 1892-1992' covering the early history of the school, and referring to one of the earlier schools held at Brook Bottom cottage, runs; *'Two sisters, the Misses Elizabeth and Sarah Harrison took over the school. One of these ladies was blind and the other partially sighted. Before coming to the village they had lived in Edenfield where their brother Joseph had a school. Joseph, however, gave up his teaching in favour of horticulture and became an expert on the cultivation of rhubarb. "Walves Noted Rhubarb" was advertised for sale at the roadside near the site of the Harrison's cottage.'*

Proceeding westerly along Ramsbottom Road towards the Bull's Head there is a property on the right, No 48 Ramsbottom Road, which was marked on the 1850 OS Map. It started life as two cottages, but converted to the current single residence No 48 and garage at a later date.

On the same side nearer the Walves Reservoir is a terrace of four cottages which again were marked on the 1850 OS Map. The last property towards the reservoir, the subject of a land lease dated 25th August 1823, was originally built as a pair of cottages which were converted to a single residence after 1919.

Looking at the central area farms, on the westerly side, we have Temple Farm which appears to have been formed as a separate holding from the previous Pelton Fold or Meadowcrofts land in the late 1700s. John Cooper and family farmed Temple during 1841, 51 and 61 with a lodger labourer, but in 1871 and 81 it was occupied by Thomas Williams, a carter, and William Stones, a farm labourer. The acreages mentioned varied between 6 and 13 acres.

Up a lane opposite Pelton Green we have Old Barn, or Higher Barn, with small acreages of 19 to 21 acres and formed as a separate farmstead in the late 1700s. James Whalley was noted as farmer here in 1841, 51, 61 and 71 with Thomas Briggs taking over in 1881.

William Kingsley, the noted Edgworth local historian wrote in 1903, *'Alfred Isherwood (son of Harry o' th' Sandy Bank) said a certain place in Quarlton near Old Ben Lane was a famous place for fisticuffs, cock fighting and bull baiting. A public house stood near (probably the Farmers' Arms on Bury Road). There were tiers for seats round this natural ampitheatre. The site has now almost disappeared by farmers livestock working the soil in'.*

Along Old Ben Lane, at a junction with the occupation lane to Higher (or Old) Barn and Sheepcote, is Old Heys. The 1850 OS Map records one building, then ruinous. The 1851 Census lists John Rostron, a 70 year old farmer with Mary Nuttall as a cotton weaver' while the 1861 Census notes Edward Entwistle a labourer as head of the household with a daughter Mary as a handloom weaver. As there are no more records of this farm, it would seem that it finished its days as a loomshop in the 1850s.

North of Old Heys is New Heys, a holding formed in the second half of the 1700s, probably by absorbing part of the Old Heys land. Access would originally have been from Old Ben Lane but after the Edgworth Enclosures in 1795 a separate access was constructed along the Quarlton Brook to Lumsgate. New Heys was farmed by Samuel Horrocks in 1841, James Greenhalgh in 1851 with 43 acres and Andrew Waddicor in 1861. There seems to have been a mix-up between Old Heys, ruinous in 1871, and New Heys when John Brooks farmed there and Elizabeth Entwistle and family were at 'Hay Farm House' (probably New Heys) in 1881.

Wickenlow, a farm on the 1620 map of the Bartons, seems to have two farmhouses in 1841 as well as a cottage. John Knowles aged 34 with wife Ann and family had one farm and James Knowles aged 35 with wife Ann and son John had the other; James Pilkington and family were in the cottage. By 1851 John Knowles was still farming there with 24 acres but James had died and the second farm was run by his widow Ann with 56 acres. In 1861 however, Wickenlow was occupied by Bennet Lee, a farm labourer. It was a single farm run by Henry Barnes with 81 acres in 1871 and by James Entwistle in 1881.

South-west of Wickenlow is Red Head or Red Earth farm formed in the mid 1600s. Prior to the recent renovation of the building, there was an old date-stone of 1660 set upside down as a quoin in the barn, but sadly lost. The description 'Red' is probably indicative of iron-oxide in the rock strata which produces a red coloration. At the auction held at the Bank Inn, Bolton, on 11th July 1827 was Lot 3, *'Red Head. Beneficial interest life of John Mason. Occupier John Hutton, farmhouse, outbuildings and 26 Cheshire acres. Rent payable almost £50 pa. and Mr Mason's life is insured in sum of £300 in respect of this property'.* Red Earth is occupied by a labourer, Richard Hamer in 1841 and uninhabited in 1851. However, an advertisement to let on 26th January 1856 was made for *'Red Earth and Morgan Tower situate in Quarlton, containing 38a 0r 28p. Cheshire acres now in occupation of Robert and James Holding. Refer to John Wilson, Kershaw's Farm, Horwich'.* By 1861, James Ollerenshaw was described as farm bailiff and was farm bailiff at Quarlton Fold in 1871. William Entwistle farmed Red Earth in 1871 and 1881. Henry Stephenson in his diary of 1878 wrote that he had seen a horse-gin in use at Red Head driving the churn and washing machine - an early form of mechanisation used to power all manner of equipment.

To the north of Wickenlow is Barons Farm, one of only two Quarlton farms owned independently of the Wright family. At the time of the Edgworth Enclosure in 1795, Barons was owned by Henry Entwistle who, as a freeholder, was entitled to an enclosure award. He received an award of 0a 3r 16p, on the 2nd June 1800, of land located over the Quarlton Brook on the west side of the Barons boundary. An access road was agreed through the newly formed Wickenlow Hill farm from

The 'Red Lion' from Ramsbottom Road c1980.

Aerial view of the 'Red Lion' and cottages c1980.

the Lumsgate Highway (Plantation Road). Barons was at this time occupied by James Barlow and later James Hutchinson. On the 9th January 1808, Barons was sold by Henry Entwistle to George Turner, a yeoman of Tottington whose estate, through Richard Brownlow and Richard Pilkington (probably trustees), sold the farm to Rivington School Governors on 15th January, 1818.

Rivington Grammar School (before it merged with Blackrod Grammar School in 1875) was endowed with land and property in the Durham area by Bishop Pilkington in 1574. The Grammar School received benefit from these properties but eventually, because of their remoteness, found difficulties in control and collecting rents. These difficulties increased until in the 1790s the Governors decided to sell off their 'North Lands'. The proceeds of sales were, over the period 1807 to 1827, invested in lands nearer home, Rivington, Heath Charnock, Over Darwen, Turton, Wheelton and Quarlton. It is, however, noted in the History of Rivington Grammar School, *'The Governors still had minor difficulties with the new tenants over non-payment of rents - especially over a farm called Barons in Quarlton.'*

Continuing difficulties led them to dispose of Barons and at an auction at the Swan Hotel, Bolton on 21st May, 1874 the governors of Rivington Grammar School sold the farm to Dr William Horrocks of Turton.

The Census Return for 1841 shows Thomas Entwistle as the farmer at Barons but from then on to 1881 no farmer is noted. In 1851 there are two families resident, James Isherwood (26) and possibly his father and mother, James (68) and Betty Isherwood. The men are both described as quarrymen. James Marsden, a farm labourer is noted in 1861 as is John Whitehead in 1871 and Richard Singleton in 1881.

We have two farms in the north, both on Moor Bottom Road leading round the contours to Holcombe from the new Crowthorn Highway built with the Edgworth Enclosure. Longshaw Head, the most northerly, and just over 1000 ft above sea level, was established in the late 1600s. Locals inform me there was a date-stone of 1713 on the farmhouse before demolition. This was the home of John Knowles, who married Ann Isherwood at Bolton Parish Church in 1803 and was the farmer in 1841 and 1851. John's widow, Ann, continued with the farm in 1861 even though 78 years old, helped by her son Andrew. 1871 saw Edmund Entwistle as the farmer of 57 acres followed by Joseph Entwistle in 1881.

The other farm along Moor Bottom Road is Morgan Tower which in 1841 was held by Henry Knowles, a stonemason, and in 1851 by Henry, now a farmer of 19 acres. There are no further records and by 1871 it appears that the larger Longshaw Head Farm incorporated the few acres of Morgan Tower. The farmhouse had become ruinous and eventually disappeared by 1908. The last evidence seen was by local historian Mr E Longworth being the gate-posts at the Tottington border with the lettering RK carved in relief in a circle. The names Morgan Tower and Maken Tower are intriguing and put down to local feeling about this isolated farmstead being similar to Malkin Tower in the Pendle Witch country.

The early 1800s were difficult years for everyone. Quarlton changed from a purely agricultural community into a mixed economy with the Industrial Revolution bringing labour intensive mills and making the domestic handloom weaving obsolete. Coal mining and quarrying expanded, new roads made transport of goods easier and encouraged the building of hamlets along their routes.

Quarlton's population in 1801 was 238 souls, with increases to 295 in 1811, 320 in 1821, 376 in 1831 and 370 in 1841, gradually reducing and stabilising at about 250 in 1891.

Local administration began to change with the establishing of the Bolton Poor Law Union in 1837, of which Quarlton Township was a member. It is interesting to mention a Bolton Journal report of the Quarlton Vestry Meeting on April 1st 1871. *'Quarlton Vestry Meeting held at the house of Mr Urmston, the Red Lion Inn. Present. Charles Whowell (Chairman), George Walker, Richard Orrell, Nathan and James Walker, James Ollerenshaw (representing J F D'arcy Wright) and John Wood, assistant Overseer. Agreed following recommendations to the Magistrates Court for appointment of Overseers; George Walker, Manufacturer; Richard Orrell, Engineer; Charles Whowell, Bleacher; Joseph Cooke, Manufacturer and William Entwistle, Farmer. Reported receipts £173.1s.0d. Expenses £159.19s.10d. Joseph Cooke the Surveyor and for next year William Entwistle appointed Surveyor at £3 pa. From rental of Township £1,387-12s-6d. Area of 798 acres.'*

The Turton Local Sanitary Board was formed in 1872 to enforce control and improvements to health standards; the area covered included Quarlton Township. They followed up medical reports of dangerous and contagious diseases and one such example arose in April 1886 when the local Inspector, James Taylor, reported on the possible causes of a family in Lodge End Cottages suffering from typhoid fever. Another two cases were reported in November 1888 at Lodge End which Dr Barr felt was caused by the unsatisfactory state of the water supply. Apparently notice was served on the owner to provide a better supply, who, to comply with the notice, fixed a tub near to a small spring on the hillside behind the house and fed water to the house by an iron pipe. The doctor found that the householders had been using the earlier supply from a spout on the roadside because they *'fancied it was better than from the tap in the house'*. The Inspector cautioned them against using the water again for domestic purposes.

The Guardians of the Poor Law Union had authority to deal with poor relief and to erect a Workhouse which they did in 1861 at Fishpool, Farnworth. The Rural Sanitary Board also had responsibilities as did the School Board. Annual rates were levied on the township residents which, for Quarlton in 1891 were two shillings in the pound of rateable value. In October 1891, notice was served that the rate levied would be increased to three shillings in the pound. Quarlton residents submitted a petition of objection to the Local Government Board saying there was only one pauper in the Township and no sanitary arrangements. The Board promptly returned the petition to the Rural Sanitary Board as the collection agency for observation and justification. The Rural Sanitary Board justified their levy noting that the Poor Law Guardians wanted £105, the Rural Sanitary Board £43, the School Board £7-10s, which together with the Overseers expenses of £10, totalled £168-10s. The rateable value is £1,258 and a rate of 3s in the pound produces £188, but about 10% would be unrecoverable through empty property, etc.

The petition is particularly interesting, giving all the interested parties' names, occupations and addresses:

Alfred Glaister	*Bleacher & Farmer*	*Quarlton Fold Farm*
William Entwistle	*Farmer*	*Red Earth Farm*
Thomas Robinson	*Farmer*	*Wickenlow Farm*
John Knowles	*Farmer*	*Higher Barn Farm*
James Greenhalgh	*Publican*	*Red Lion Inn*
William Ollerenshaw	*Farm Bailiff*	*Pelton Fold Farm*
(for Mrs J C Wright)		
Jacob Horrocks	*Finisher*	*68 Quarlton*
Thomas Snape	*Finisher*	*16 Quarlton*
Robert Suthurst	*Labourer*	*85 Quarlton*
Thomas Haworth	*Printer*	*83 Quarlton*
Turner Turner	*Slater*	*78 Quarlton*
James Greenhalgh	*Weaver*	*72 Quarlton*
John Greenhalgh	*Labourer*	*74 Quarlton*
Eliza Butterworth	*Housekeeper*	*70 Quarlton*
Elizabeth Mills	*Housekeeper*	*48 Quarlton*
Joseph Harrison	*Gardener*	*10 Quarlton*
John Howarth	*????*	*14 Quarlton*
Sarah Harrison	*Housekeeper*	*75 Quarlton*
William Lexter	*Labourer*	*62 Quarlton*
John Fletcher	*Stonebreaker*	*Quarlton*
Jane Haslam	*Housekeeper*	*87 Quarlton*

Thomas Cotton	*Labourer*	*46 Quarlton*
Richard Ramwell	*Farmer*	*Top o' the Quarlton*
Thomas Foster	*Contractor*	*Walves*
John Thomas Howarth	*Printer*	*64 Walves*
William Mather	*Cloth Looker*	*84 Walves*
Richard Mather	*Machine Printer*	*82 Quarlton*
Thomas Howarth	*Stone Mason*	*84 Quarlton*
Rebecca Howarth	*None*	*76 Quarlton*

Turton Urban District Council was formed in 1872 and enlarged to include Bradshaw and Harwood in 1898;- its final form to last until reorganisation in 1974. Turton UDC took over the responsibilities for all local requirements of seven townships including Quarlton.

Quarlton was one of the townships making up the ancient Parish of Bolton-le- Moors until the foundation of the Parish of Turton and building of St Annes Church in 1841, when Quarlton became part of the new Turton Parish. Quarlton folk continued, however, to worship, have baptisms, marriages and burials at Turton and Holcombe as well as Tottington, whichever was most convenient, or where they had family ties. This state of affairs also applied to the nearby areas of Tottington Lower End and Hawkshaw Lane and as Hawkshaw village itself grew, the need for a local church became justifiable. The new Church of St Mary's, Hawkshaw was consecrated in 1892. Their new parish included the parts of Quarlton in the Walves area up to the Walves Reservoir following the Township boundary and Old Ben Lane, across to the easterly boundary of Quarlton at Clough Bottom. This meant that all the Walves Cottages, Knotts, Quarlton Fold, Top of Quarlton, Lower Fold and the Delph Cottages were now members of the new Chapelry of St Mary's, Hawkshaw. Quarlton children attended either the Edgworth Methodist Schools or St Mary's Church of England School at Hawkshaw, whichever was in easy reach.

Chapter VIII   THE TWENTIETH CENTURY

The Holcombe Hunt enjoyed continuing prosperity at the turn of the century under the Master, Thomas Hardcastle of Bradshaw Hall (1899-1902) who was followed by his son as Master, Henry M Hardcastle (1903-1919), also of Bradshaw Hall.

The Hunt's established use of Quarlton was inhibited by lease changes in the last quarter of the 19th Century. John Jackson, huntsman from 1867 to 1899, wrote in his reminiscences (1901) that they had the right to hunt six days a season in Quarlton, although earlier Mr Wright hunted over it and latterly *'Alfred Glaister of Mill Hill Bleachworks, Bolton, got the place and preserved rabbits'*. Before this John Jackson says *'it used to be the best hunting ground we had'*. When meeting in the area the Hunt met at the Bull's Head or the Wagon and Horses at Hawkshaw.

The 1914/18 War brought much misery and sorrow to all Britain with great loss of life affecting every town and village. Even from the small group of Walves Cottages six men lost their lives. The neighbouring Holcombe Moor Military Training Area was a constant reminder of military activity and Meadowcroft's Farm fields were used in 1914/15, along with Sharples Meadow, for the encampments of troops preparing for the Gallipoli Campaign in Turkey.

The Holcombe Moor Training Area established in the 1860s was initially laid out using the valley bottom of the Red Brook and Holcombe Brook up to and including Bull Hill. At a later date, additional areas were leased for limited manoeuvres on Quarlton Heights and parts of Longshaw Head, Red Head and Top of Quarlton.

Early in the 1900s, James Greenhalgh, the long time publican of the Red Lion, sold his public house and bowling green to the Crown Brewery of Magee Marshall and Co Ltd of Bolton. This south-eastern corner of Quarlton became more reliant on the industries, churches, chapels and social life of Hawkshaw as time went on and to many people the Walves cottages and Ramsbottom Road merged into the hamlet of Hawkshaw. The new Walves Bridge over the brook was built in 1900. The Quarlton Manor, having been owned by only three families since 1600, the Radcliffes, the Bartons and the Wrights, the status quo was about to change. Henry Wright died 24th November 1864 leaving his estates in trust to his daughter Julia Catherine, wife of James Frederick D'arcy and her sons and daughters on condition that their husbands adopted the name of Wright as their main surname. On 4th June 1884, Julia Mary Catherine Wright, only child of Julia Catherine Wright, married Edward Withenden Curteis, who died 25th February 1902. Julia Mary Catherine Wright later married Aubrey Beaumont Wallis. Mother, Julia Catherine Wright, died on 31st May 1916 and soon after her son-in-law, Henry Aubrey Beaumont Wallis, changed his surname to Wright.   It was decided to sell the Quarlton Estate, the vendor being Mrs Julia Mary Catherine Wallis-Wright.

The public auction was arranged for 4.0pm (prompt) on Thursday, 20th November, 1919 at the Pack Horse Hotel, Bolton to be conducted by Lomax, Sons and Mills. It was advertised as being *'Twelve Excellent Dairy Farms, Accommodation and Building Lands, Reservoir, Water Rights and Well-secured Ground Rents being in Edgworth, Quarlton, Bradshaw and Turton, comprising an area of over 863 acres'* as follows:

Lot 1	*Chief Rents on land including the Red Lion and attached four cottages together with the freehold on the Bowling Green land. In occupation of Crown Brewery Co Ltd.*
Lot 2	*Ground Rent on 3 houses and shop Nos 71 to 77 Bolton Road,*
Lot 3	*Freehold on 1½ acres land on south side of Ramsbottom Road.*
Lots 4-10	*Land and ground rents in Bradshaw.*
Lot 11	*Quarlton Fold Farm, Lower House Farm (Lower Fold) and Walves Reservoir. 238 acres.0.22 of land and 8 acres.1.13 of water. In the occupation of John Bostock. Ground rents were included in this lot for Walves cottages and Saltpie.*
Lots 12 & 13	*Ground rents for Lodge End cottages.*
Lots 14 & 15	*Refer to Birches farms in Bradshaw.*
Lot 16	*Pallet farm, together with Knott's cottage, 46 acres.0.30. In the occupation of Mr Edward Winder.*
Lot 17	*Pelton Fold Farm. 41 acrea.0.18. in occupation of Mr H P Birkett.*
Lot 18	*Ground rent on Pelton Green. House and garden, Mr T Greenhalgh.*
Lot 19	*Higher Barn Farm. 46 acres.2.19. Occupied by Mr Syddle.*
Lot 20 & 21	*Chief and Ground rents on Bury Road cottages.*
Lot 22	*Temple Farm. 12 acres.3.20. In the occupation of Mr W Isherwood.*
Lot 23	*New Heys Farm. 43 acres.3.39. Occupied by Miss A Entwistle.*
Lot 24 & 25	*Sandy Bank and Wickenlow Hill farms in Edgworth.*
Lot 26	*Wickenlow Farm. 80 acres.0.10. In the occupation of Mr P Dearden.*
Lot 27	*Longshaw Head. 34 acres.2.9. In the occupation of Mr S Howarth.*
Lot 28	*Quarlton Heights land (44 acres) not included in sale*
Lot 29	*Quarlton Vale Print Works. Occupied by Mr T E Clarke.*
Lots 30-32	*Ground Rents on land of Printers Row and gardens etc.*
Lots 33 & 34	*Ground Rents on land of Vale Cotton Mill, Turton Bottoms and Vale House.*
Lot 35	*Land adjacent to old Paper Mill, Turton. (Jumbles)*
Lot 36	*Ground Rent on plot of land forming part of Edgworth Recreation Ground lake. (Quarlton side)*

In the event only one Edgworth farm and several ground rents were auctioned. However Mr Frederick Whowell bought Top of Quarlton, and Red Earth farms prior to the auction, on 5th September 1918 and Wickenlow, Lower Fold and Longshaw Head afterwards on 10th June 1920. These purchases also included the old Maken Tower land, the farmhouse and buildings then being ruinous.

Mr Frederick Whowell was the son of Charles Whowell who acquired Two Brooks Bleachworks in 1850, having previously been a manager at Hardcastle's Bradshaw Hall Bleachworks. Frederick Whowell took charge of the Two Brooks Works on the death of his father Charles. In 1900 the Bleachers' Association, of which Charles Whowell Ltd was a member, formed a Limited Company with the object of amalgamating member firms into one concern. Although part of the Bleachers' Asociation Ltd from 1900, Two Brooks Bleachworks continued to operate under the name of Charles Whowell Ltd with a local director. Frederick Whowell became a Director of the Bleachers' Association and later one of the joint Managing Directors. Two Brooks Works finally closed in 1937. Frederick Whowell, very much the Squire of Hawkshaw, had interests that included half of Quarlton. He died January 5th 1927, a much respected industrialist and personality of the area.

Apart from the purchase of Temple Farm by Joseph Ramwell in 1920, the other Quarlton farms continued to be tenanted until sold at various times by the Wright Estate right up to the 1970s.

Just after the Great War of 1914-18, when petrol engined vehicles were starting to take over from horse-drawn traffic, a small transport concern, Taylor Bros, was established at No 48, Ramsbottom Road, that became known as Tunnel Garage. Brothers George, Edgar, Fred and Tom started a bus service from Holcombe Brook to the Royal Oak at Bradshaw Brow where it met the electric tram. This ran until 1922 when the route was taken over by the Ribble Bus Co. The Taylor brothers continued for some time with charabancs for trips and excursions: the Tunnel Garage was given its name because of the old coal drift or sough sited in the hillside behind the house.

Apart from small scale forays into the old workings during the 1926 miners' strike there had been no organised coal mining since the closure of the old Quarlton Colliery. However, the quarries enjoyed periodic revivals; the long established quarry adjacent to the old Quarlton Colliery site was worked in the 1930s with delivery lorries using Coal Pit Lane. The last large scale quarrying was on land at Wickenlow north of the farm when shales were taken for brickmaking by Joseph Higson and Co, who operated their 'Higson's Machine Brickworks' at Bella Street, Daubhill. This continued over a three year period just before and during World War II.

The Quarlton and Edgworth districts have always been much appreciated walking areas of the Bolton and Bury industrial workers who relished the fresh air of the uplands. In 1928 this encouraged the Trustees of 'Bury Schools Holiday Camps' to buy Red Earth Farm with a covenant that it could only be used for *'convalescent and recreational purposes'*. The Trustees sold the property back to private ownership in 1939 for fringe farming activity. This part of Quarlton was also used by the Bolton

Boy Scout Association who had an encampment area with a 'Guest House' near the Quarlton Brook adjacent to Wickenlow Hill Farm.

For over a hundred years the Quarlton farmers had been stock rearing and fattening cattle and sheep, with those at the lower levels going for the local milk trade - well able to supply the needs of the local industrial towns. The 1939-45 War brought quite an upheaval in local farming practice with the local War Agricultural Committee dictating what was to be done for the War effort. The Quarlton farmers had to return to the old traditional mixed farming and most of the farmers were expected to grow cereals. Mr Lee Ramwell of Wickenlow Hill farm, at that time having most of the Wickenlow and Longshaw Head land, grew 25-30 acres of barley as well as fields of kale and turnips. The implements were provided by the War Agricultural Committee and seasonal help came from Land Army Girls and Italian Prisoners of War who were camped at Bury. Growing a barley crop at nearly 1000 feet above sea level cannot have been easy, but needs must.

The water supply to these upland regions was always a problem but with the improving standards of public health, many local wells became unsuitable and in some cases dangerous. The Walves cottages were fed by a mains supply from Tottington / Ramsbottom early in the 1900s, but the Bury Road cottages got their piped supply in November 1941. The cost of laying the three inch main was £700, each property having to bear a proportional part of the cost according to potential usage, allowing for a TUDC share of 45%. It is interesting to note that Temple Farm was then owned by Elizabeth Ellen Halliday, Meadowcrofts Farm and Cottage by Lady Nina Knowles, but Pelton Fold Farm, Pallet Farm and Cottage still belonged to the Wright Estate.

Being in the flight path for bombers attacking Manchester and Liverpool, there were many German planes flying over our area. Bombs and incendiaries were jettisoned after an abortive attack on 18th October 1940, one stick falling in a line over Affetside, Two Brooks and Top of Quarlton, thankfully with no casualties but with some property damage and livestock loss. In December 1944, Manchester was attacked by air-launched VI Flying Bombs, some falling short, one in particular doing great damage in Tottington when a terrace of cottages was demolished with a loss of seven lives. One such VI also landed in Quarlton just south-east of Red Earth Farm making a 12-15 foot crater on open land about 6 feet deep; nearby buildings were also affected. Propaganda leaflets were found in the area, the containers of which were impelled from the bomb on its final dive to the ground.

With the end of the War in 1945, Quarlton life settled back into its old pattern - still largely agricultural, but with the pre-war closure of Two Brooks Bleachworks, locals had to travel out of the area for employment. After the early post war years of austerity,

Taylor Brothers' coach with a local excursion party, c1920.

Bomb damage to Top of Quarlton Barn, 18th October 1940.

Crater caused by a V1 Flying Bomb, south-east of Red Earth, looking towards the Grainings, December 1944.

motor cars became available and responsible Councils looked at their main access roads. Turton Urban District Council put forward a scheme to straighten out the section of Bury Road passing close to Temple Farm, and the necessary piece of Pelton Fold Farm was bought on 23rd December 1958. The new road took a fairly straight line from Pelton Green to south-east of the bridge over Walleach Brook. The northerly section of the old road was left as access to Temple Farm.

Before the 1939-45 War the only farms to be sold from the Wright Estate were those bought by Frederick Whowell, ie Top of Quarlton, Lower Fold, Red Earth, Wickenlow and the old Maken Tower land. After the war the remaining farms were sold off by the Wright Estate Trustees including Knotts in 1948 to Mr J E Hope, Pelton Fold in 1951 to Mr Thomas Dewhurst, Higher Barn in 1954 to Mr Charles Halliday, Pallet in 1962 to Mr William Ramwell and Quarlton Fold in 1971 to Mr Herbert W Ramwell.

Continuing grazing by sheep and cattle has maintained the Quarlton character with its landscape of broad hills and slopes, but a recent change has been the purchase of ten acres by Lancashire County Council from the Lower Fold land of Mr and Mrs J Tetlow in 1963 to enable planting of coniferous forestry, now well established. Similarly Mr Clive Holker of Red Earth Farm has planted a substantial boundary of trees around his nursery land.

Most of Quarlton's farmhouses have now been renovated into desirable residences with little or no farming activity. Quarlton Fold however, farmed by Herbert Ramwell and his son John, is still wholly agricultural, with sheep and cattle grazing over a large acreage. Temple is worked by the Figgins family but the current economic difficulties with agriculture has necessitated some diversification. Red Earth and Temple Farms operate horticultural nurseries while Wickenlow - renamed Quarlton Manor Farm - and Pelton Fold offer visiting guest facilities.

The Red Lion Hotel, after an almost complete rebuild, flourishes as a restaurant/public house with accommodation, initially under the ownership of Jennings Bros, plc, Castle Brewery of Cockermouth. All the roadside properties have been generally upgraded and are well in demand as country residences by people employed in Bolton and Bury. The few new buildings built in Quarlton in the last hundred years or so include the new Quarlton Fold farmhouse and the five large residences built on the site of the old Quarlton Print Works.

Quarlton Township maintains its semi-moorland character and continues to offer a good life for its two hundred or so residents while pleasing visitors from the towns with the many footpaths over the hills offering the most fantastic views in the area.

Terrace adjacent to the Red Lion built in 1910 replacing four previous cottages built in 1826.

The new Quarlton Fold Farmhouse in 1999.

A new housing development, 'Quarlton Gardens' on the site of Quarlton Vale Printworks, built in 1989-97.

Quarlton's Twentieth Century buildings.

Mr Frederick Whowell who, in 1918, bought Top of Quarlton, Makin Tower Longshaw Head, Red Earth, Wickenlow and Lower Fold from the Wright Estate.

The Two-Brooks Football Team with Mr F Whowell. The Whowells established Two Brooks Bleachworks in 1850 and ran the company until closure in 1937.

BIBLIOGRAPHY

1 Victoria County History of Lancashire
2 Clitheroe Court Rolls 1504-67   Transcribed William Farrer   1913
3 The Holcombe Hunt   A N Walker   1937
4 Holcombe Long Ago   Rev H Dowsett   1901
5 Notes on Holcombe   Rev H Dowsett   1902
6 Historical Notices of Helmshore & Musbury P Stephen & R Hawkin   1927
7 History of Bolton   J C Scholes   1892
8 Historical Gleanings of Bolton & District   B T Barton   1881
9 History of Smithills Families   Marie Mitchell   1991
10 Tottington Lower End Survey   1794
11 Edgworth Enclosure Act   1795
12 Little Bolton-Edenfield Turnpike Act   1797
13 Orders & Proceedings of the Turnpike Trustees   1797-1817
14 Lancashire Families   Edward Baines   1893
15 Genealogy of the Knowles Family   James C Scholes   1886
16 Scowcroft Diaries   1812-1907
17 Edgworth & District Agricultural Society 21st Show Souvenir   1909
18 History of Rivington & Blackrod Grammar School   M M Kay   1931
19 St Mary's, Hawkshaw 1892-1992   H Bragg & J R Hodson
20 Flying Bombs over the Pennines   Peter J C Smith   1988
21 Publications of Turton Local History Society   Nos 1,3,7,15,18 & 19

ACKNOWLEDGMENTS

I wish to thank the following who gave information freely relating to their properties or to Quarlton in general.

Bolton Local Studies Dept. Bolton	Jenny Hodges, Delph Cottage
Lancashire Record Office, Preston	Clive Holker, Red Earth
Jan Barnes, Hawkshaw	Eddie Longworth, Hawkshaw
Cathy Bullen, Meadowcrofts	Vera Longworth, Bromley Cross
Christine Collins, Pelton Fold	Herbert Ramwell, Quarlton Fold
Alan Davies Lancs Mining Museum	Emil Salem, Bury
Phil Davies, Wickenlow	John Simpson, Helmshore
Margaret Edlington, Bolton	N A Taylor, Meadowcrofts
Arthur Fairhurst, Tottington	Lillian Tinsley, Hawkshaw
John Firth, Top of Quarlton	Marion Thomas, Barons
Brenda Fox, Garstang	Janet Walker, Wrea Green
Harry Gibson, Lower Fold	John Watson, Cleveleys
Betty Haslam, Harwood	Mike Williams, Edgworth
Peter Harris, Bradshaw	Frederick Horridge, Harwood

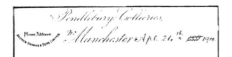

The Red Lion Hotel
at Hawkshaw

BROOKSIDE GARAGE

Proprietor : J. STEVENS

MOTOR   REPAIRS
PAINTING AND BODY
RENOVATIONS
PETROL AND OIL
CARS BOUGHT, SOLD
OR EXCHANGED

133 BURY ROAD · EDGWORTH

TELEPHONE :   TURTON 325

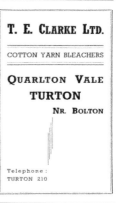

T. E. CLARKE LTD.

COTTON YARN BLEACHERS

QUARLTON VALE
TURTON
NR. BOLTON

Telephone :
TURTON 210

TEMPLE FARM NURSERIES

Lots and lots of bedding plants and hundreds of flowers to fill your garden all summer long

Bed & Breakfast

PELTON FOLD FARM
Bury Road, Edgworth, Lancashire BL7 0BS
Telephone 01204 852207

RED EARTH FARM NURSERIES

SUBSIDIARY OF C.M.HOLKER (CONSTRUCTION) LTD

Red Earth Farm, Plantation Road, Turton, Nr. Bolton, Lancs BL7 0DD
Tel: 01204 853243 Fax: 01204 853274

WITH COMPLIMENTS

Edgworth, Turton, Bolton,
Lancashire BL7 0DD
Tel: 01204 852277   Fax: 01204 852286
Mobile: 0976 535540

Quarlton Manor Farm
Country House Hotel

PUBLICATIONS OF TURTON LOCAL HISTORY SOCIETY

No 1	Stories of Turton Date Stones	R Lindop	1975
No 2	Lords of the Manor of Bradshaw	J J Francis	1977
No 3	Turton Tales (1)	R Lindop	1978
No 4	Bradshaw Works	J J Francis	1979
No 5	Bradshaw and Harwood Collieries	J J Francis	1982
No 6	The Bradshaw Flood (2nd Edition)	Rev S H Martin	1984
No 7	Enclosure of Edgworth Moor	J J Francis	1986
No 8	Turton Tales (2) G Openshaw & J G Barber-Lomax		1987
No 9	Harwood Friendly Societies	J J Francis	1987
No 10	The Bradshaw Chapel History Trail	J J Francis	1988
No 11	The History of Turton Mill	R Lindop	1989
No 12	Datestones of Bradshaw & Harwood	AS & E Day	1989
No 13	The Enclosure of Harwood Commons	J J Francis	1990
No 14	Horrobin Mill	J J Francis	1992
No 15	Affetside: An Historical Survey	J J Francis	1994
No 16	Eagley Brook: A Lancashire Stream	Helen Heyes	1997
No 17	Harwood Vale: 1865-1965	J F Horridge	1997
No 18	Bradshaw Chapel I	J J Francis	1998
No 19	Bradshaw Chapel II	J J Francis	1998
No 20	2000 - Turton through the Ages	Ed. J F Horridge	1999
No 21	Quarlton	J J Francis	2000
No 21	Quarlton 2nd Edition	J J Francis	2009
No 22	Hardy Cornmill	J F Horridge	2001
No 23	People and Places of Turton	Ed. J F Horridge	2003
No 24	Lost Industries of Turton Moor	P M Harris	2003
No 25	Harwood Hill Farms & Riding Gate	J J Francis	2004
No 26	Samuel Scowcroft's Diary	Joan Francis	2005
No 27	Harwood - The Early Years	J F Horridge	2006
No 28	Birches	J J Francis & P M Harris	2006
No 29	Turton Fair	Alec Bagley & Pat Bagley	2007
No 30	Highways of Turton	J J Francis	2007
No 31	Churches and Chapels of Turton	D J Leeming	2008
No 32	The Barlow Institute 1909-2009	J J Francis	2009
No 33	Entwistle	C R Walsh	2011
No 34	Turton Workhouse	D J Leeming	2011
No 35	The Bradshaw Estate 1542-1919	J J Francis	2012
No 36	Mining in Turton	P M Harris	2013
No 37	Pubs in Turton Part 1	John Barlow	2018
No 38	Egerton	S J Tonge	2019

Daber + Alker
Salford
Albert / Richard.

Printed in Great Britain
by Amazon